After
Account
ability

A
CRITICAL
GENEALOGY
OF A
CONCEPT

REVISED AND UPDATED EDITION

PINKO

HAYMARKET BOOKS
CHICAGO, ILLINOIS

© 2025 Pinko collective. First published by Wendy's Subway in New York in 2023.

This edition published in 2025 by
Haymarket Books
P.O. Box 180165
Chicago, IL 60618
www.haymarketbooks.org

ISBN: 979-8-88890-265-3

Distributed to the trade in the US through Consortium Book Sales and Distribution (www.cbsd.com) and internationally through Ingram Publisher Services International (www. ingramcontent.com).

This book was published with the generous support of Lannan Foundation, Wallace Action Fund, and Marguerite Casey Foundation.

Special discounts are available for bulk purchases by organizations and institutions. Please email info@ haymarketbooks.org for more information.

Cover and interior design by David Knowles.

Printed in Canada by union labor.

Library of Congress Cataloging-in-Publication data is available.

10 9 8 7 6 5 4 3 2 1

AFTER ACCOUNTABILITY
A Critical Genealogy of a Concept

I

After Account ability: An Intro duction to the Project

MOTIVATION

In the George Floyd uprising of 2020—the highest and most widespread period of revolt in living US memory—certain concepts surged up from the heaving streets and shimmered aloft for a remarkable moment, catching the eye. These were political terms drawing from carefully tended revolutionary theory and practice which suddenly gained a mass, public character. *Abolition* was one, though briskly swapped for *defund* in slogans as liberals rushed to join in. But a related word kept its air for longer: *accountability*. This term had its path prepared for it by a homologue in robust use by legal and moral discourses, but accountability in this sense was, for the mass audience, something new. Familiar to anyone participating in left politics in the last quarter century, it brought with it a particular vocabulary and set of procedures, as well as the aspiration to address those outside of radical circles. If there was a concept that spanned the knife's edge of the radical activity of the period leading up to this general revolt and the broad swing of its sudden uptake, this was it.

The concept of accountability also described the moment's limits. The uprising exceeded the capacities of any existing political organization to direct it, and the state moved to harness the rebellion for its own ends. On the one hand, it carried out a vicious display of repression, beating, gassing, kidnapping, and assassinating the participants in this unprecedented global assembly against police power; on the other, it turned to its bland, brazen style of recuperation to reassert control. The infamous photo of Nancy Pelosi kneeling in kente cloth, for example, was taken at a press conference to introduce the George Floyd Justice in Policing Act, whose first line stated its aim to "hold law enforcement accountable."

The epochal nature of the uprising was plain to all observers. But at the moment of its partisans' most dramatic turns of fortune, accountability seemed almost as often a stumbling block as an element of its sudden success. In New York City, for example, one of the largest abolitionist formations was torn apart in the heat of the summer action over a failure of accountability around sexual violence. This experience was far from unique. Across the country, and over the last several years, revolutionary organizations on all flanks of the left, from the International Socialist Organization to the Black Rose Anarchist Federation, had collided with their own inability to internally address and account for sexual assault. The widespread concurrence, it seemed, meant that this wasn't due to any one tendency's particular commitments, but instead represented a concrete political impasse. Accountability, usually in the form of its declared failure, was repeatedly at the center of debilitating crises within revolutionary political organizations.

Nevertheless, the concept continued to circulate among the left as something just short of a program, seeming to name the ache of proximity between crystalline, utopian promise and mundane, bleary failure. It was the companion of thrilling achievements of revolutionary organizing that summer, and also their collapse. Thrust into the position of tutors for an eager, inchoate movement, many abolitionists had toolkits, trainings, workshops, and infographics at the ready. Perhaps they didn't have a total strategy to hand out, but then they never said they would. In this way, they confirmed themselves as heirs of the political dilemma governing the left of the last half century.

As the uprising was bludgeoned back from the streets, the drive to understand it in relation to history became more pressing. People had to reach back to the century-cracking sequences of uprisings in the 1960s and '70s to orient themselves. Historically apt or not, this seemed to reveal a secret correspondence between the past rupture and the present that cast the intervening decades of political activity as nothing but an attempt to prepare for its return. Our collective had come together a few years earlier, partly out of a desire to restore a properly revolutionary history of concepts relating to sexual form that circulated without acknowledging this similar moment of origin. Beginning in this context, we had drawn up a list of open questions we saw in the field of queer left politics. One of these was the cluster of concepts around accountability. Every one of us had had different kinds of encounters with accountability processes in our various communities, though the way people took it up didn't indicate a clear sense of shared meaning. We recognized an impasse: frequent acrimonious conflicts between rival sides, which each had clear merits but advanced irreconcilable interpretations of the same circumstances. Were countercultural spaces and movements overly exclusionary and punitive towards those accused of harm, or overly accommodating of predatory abusers? Were the recent collapses of several political organizations, coalitions, and projects over debates about sexual violence necessary and positive steps in rooting out long-standing forms of abuse, or were they tragic losses to movement-building that could have been addressed differently?

Do our movements need more honest confrontations with conflict or more careful resolution?

These questions and others swirled around our collective and broader networks. They suggested to us the need for more theorizing, for thinking deeper and further, and perhaps for thinking laterally to existing debates. As with our approach to other questions, we wanted to draw out the lineage of these concepts and return them to their history in specific traditions of revolutionary activity and thought. As we began working on our first magazine issue, we left the complicated topic for a later date.

We had often invoked the political context of the liberation movement of the long 1960s—one of global anticolonial uprising—as having conditioned its theorization of gender and sexuality. Now an uprising seemed to have returned, and with it, the open question of accountability appeared to demand answers. We were curious about the clash between concepts and practices that had been used to sustain the memory of these uprisings throughout the decades of reaction and how they functioned now that the hoped-for moment of revolt had arrived. What had changed? What had been preserved? We wanted to hear from people who had attended the birth of these concepts in hopes of opening up a different kind of space for theorizing. To do so we needed to talk to many people, all of whom shared a long-standing commitment to thinking about accountability, but who came to it through multiple and varied paths and often arrived at quite different conclusions.

We wanted to trace links between contemporary debates about accountability and an earlier era of struggle in the 1960s and '70s. There were many possibilities; we could have sought such a genealogy through a number of varied possible lineages: the legacy of prisoner rebellions and prisoner organizing, or women's organizing against intimate-partner violence, for example. One of our editors, drawing on her own political experience, hypothesized one possible lineage connecting the New Communist Movement of the 1970s to abolitionist organizations of the 2000s.

Militants of the mid-1970s witnessed both mass insurgency and movements confronting their limits—in state repression, in economic crisis, and in the ebb of broad participation. They saw the problem as how to articulate the overabundant energies of the varied fronts of self-liberation into an effective political formation before the moment passed. There were many valiant attempts. The Black Panthers may have squared this circle theoretically, but after their strangulation, some of those who were left in the New Communist Movement spent the next decade attempting to forge the proper line that would galvanize a steadily aging mass of radicals into a party.

The New Communist Movement was the name given to political activity taken by a major current of New Left radicals and others in the 1970s. Drawing inspiration from the Chinese, Cuban, and Vietnamese revolutions, they sought to find a new path to communism in the United States. Guided by what they understood of Mao and the Chinese critique of Soviet communism, they attempted to turn the popular forms of struggle against US hegemony into an organization that could exceed the role played by the diminished and discredited Communist Party of the United States of America (CPUSA). These militants saw themselves as "anti-revisionist," returning to a Marxist-Leninist politics prior to a perceived deterioration by Soviet bureaucracy. This political formation barely survived the Reaganite counterrevolution of the 1980s, sustaining famished traditions of struggle in various states of open militancy and disguise.

There were reasons for us to hypothesize that the New Communist Movement of the 1970s had contributed to iterations of the concept of accountability in the 2000s. Accountability as put forth by abolitionist or transformative justice thinking shared some resemblance to "criticism/self-criticism" that characterized the Maoist movements of the '70s and '80s. These were remembered pejoratively as "struggle sessions"—moments of collective abuse or self-abasement, used as a metonym for the internal antagonism that seemed to limit the movement as a whole; but at their most commendable, they represented a disciplined commitment to revolutionary conduct at all times. These parallels were not just conceptual. Militants influenced by the earlier era of the New Communist Movement had participated in the formation of a number of influential nonprofits in the '90s and 2000s. This influence, one of our editors hypothesized, might have hinged on the organization Critical Resistance. Founded by Angela Davis and Ruth Wilson Gilmore with others in the late '90s, Critical Resistance and associated formations bridged revolutionary elders from the previous cycles of struggles and the newer engagement with notions of accountability.

We were curious to explore this possible relation of accountability to this earlier attempt at revolutionary party formation, as part of a broader inquiry into the genealogy of contemporary concepts of accountability.

We took up this possible link to the New Communist Movement as one way into a broader research question on the origins and meanings of accountability as a movement concept. We hoped historicizing the concept in movement history would provide a way through what often seemed to be an impasse in its application. The recent career of the concepts associated with accountability—their wide adoption and ambivalent success at resolving sexual assault, abuse, and harm within political communities—might, we thought, be made clearer if we approached the tools used from a historical entry point. At the very least, we hoped we could discover a minor red thread, tracing a pathway from the explosion of the '60s through the various scattered scenes, projects, traditions, and institutions it left deposited across the US landscape through a long period of defeat until now.

We studied some of the literature on the New Communist Movement and the eloquent accounts that transformative justice and abolitionist organizations had written of themselves, and discussed what we knew of the evolution of the concept of accountability. We compiled a list of transformative justice practitioners, abolitionist and communist organizers, queer and feminist community pillars, and others to interview, all representing different tendencies, histories, and approaches to accountability. We were unsuccessful in reaching every one of them, but in the end we were able to speak with members of the communist pre-party formations, Critical Resistance, Survived & Punished, Bash Back!, incarcerated and criminalized thinkers and revolutionaries, and movement professionals.

The interviews were primarily conducted over the course of a few months in spring and summer of 2021, when the George Floyd uprising was still a fresh memory but people hadn't been on the streets for nearly a year. One interview took place later, in 2024. Some interviews were held in person and some over the phone or Zoom, and one through an electronic prison messaging system. A residency we had been awarded provided funds for transcription and honoraria for the interviewees, though most refused payment. Collective members were paired with some interview subjects they knew. Generally, these relationships were from previous periods of organizing, or between people who had neither organized nor been in community with each other for several years. As such, the interviewees are remarkably candid about the histories, limitations, and disappointments they link with the concepts associated with accountability.

We trained ourselves in oral-history interview practices and drew up a standard question sheet for every interview to follow, but planned for the conversations to flow organically. We posed the interview as one interested in the concept pair of "failure" and "accountability," which we thought would invite a more open, critical reflection than a boosterish presentation of the tradition. We asked practitioners to place themselves in a political lineage, personally and organizationally, and to share how they thought the concept had evolved.

Of course, however alluring, concepts do not act on their own. They are the product of people thinking, criticizing, remembering, fighting, and passing down elements of their concrete situation in history and struggle. But as one of the interviewees notes, some concepts have a strange, self-reflexive aspect. The ways people analyze power when attempting to intervene in a specific political situation form a condition of what is possible to do within that situation itself. The concepts leave their mark on what people are capable of carrying out. This endows them, reciprocally, with a special openness to history, and makes them a sensitive register and arena of political struggles.

What we found in this investigation was a marked overlap in terms of individual political trajectories, continuity of scenes, basic practices, and terms. But it's also clear that, when comparing the responses of older militants to those with a more direct hand in the formation of contemporary transformative justice thinking, the concepts and traditions referred to do not precisely coincide. Rather than unearthing a concealed history of the '60s in the present, the responses we got from interviewees offer extremely rich reflections on the shared political dilemmas, limits, and divergent strategies that accountability was developed to address. Each of the interviewees have insightful, striking things to say about their practice and their understanding of its history. For now, an introduction and overview of the interviewees and their rough sketch of the history of the concept's trajectory will give a sense of what we learned, which we present as a series of oppositions that structure the field of their thought.

POLITICAL ORIGINS

Esteban Kelly describes his political trajectory as stemming from an adolescence in the mid-'90s New York City punk scene and its political institutions: Food Not Bombs, migrant solidarity, Zapatista and Mumia support, and Green Scare anti-repression campaigns. His first paid organizing job was as a peer sex educator for a nonprofit's queer youth program, which meant tabling at punk shows to hand out condoms. He was exposed to an older generation of radical thinking through a Long Island anarchist collective where he was given the likes of Silvia Federici, Midnight Notes, and Harry Cleaver to read.

After college at UC Berkeley, where he was involved with the Black Panther Commemoration Committee and the housing co-op world, he moved to Philadelphia in 2004 and was immediately recruited to a new collective, Philly Stands Up, which had formed following a sexual assault at a punk music fest. This collective had been organized by a survivor support group called Philly's Pissed to work directly with men as an affiliate, but soon after this group grasped that it would mean challenging their friends—men who held social status in the scene—the numbers dropped from thirty to three. Esteban joined right after this winnowing, which he saw as an opportunity for the group to take itself seriously and actually commit to the mandate of holding perpetrators accountable.

Some of Philly Stands Up's procedures were semi-acknowledged inheritances from '60s-era formations like the Movement for a New Society, a Quaker antiwar activist network that populated the local horizon—decision by consensus, points of unity, etc. Not everyone was trained in them. Over the following years, the makeup of the group shifted from being mostly in the punk community to being in the queer community to being QTPOC-led. Around this same time, a member's partner mentioned that the group's practices resembled something they'd been reading about—transformative justice (TJ). The group began studying existing TJ as a way of explaining to themselves what they felt they were already doing. After a few years of operation, they linked up with a wider national scene working on TJ at the 2010 Allied Media conference. This formation was already semi-professionalized, had one foot in academia and one in nonprofit grant land, and they invited Philly Stands Up to join in the national network.

——

Emi Kane describes INCITE! as a collective prominent in left circles, stemming from a 2000 conference at UC Santa Cruz called by women of color organizing against police brutality and sexual violence. The group's founders felt there was a lack of gender analysis in anti-police brutality movements and a lack of racial-justice analysis in struggles against sexual violence, exemplified by white carceral feminist frameworks for responding to sexual violence. What INCITE! provided was an analysis that grasped the connection between state and interpersonal violence. It functioned as a national organizing collective with local chapters and affiliated organizations, never incorporating as a 501(c)(3). Some campaigns took place outside of the US, in Canada and in the Navajo Nation. Emi sees that its utility was to provide a place for advancing analysis and political education rather than serve as a mobilizing project. INCITE! partnered with Critical Resistance to cohere and share analysis across the movement, though at present it is no longer as active.

———

Hyejin Shim places herself in INCITE!'s lineage, as many of the organizers who formed Survived & Punished met at the 2015 Color of Violence 4 conference that INCITE! organized. At the time, Hyejin was leading a defense campaign to support an undocumented survivor of abuse and attended the conference for a discussion by people working on the defense campaign for Marissa Alexander, a woman fighting incarceration for having fired a warning shot at her abusive husband. Previously, Hyejin had worked at an Asian women's shelter for queer and trans immigrant and refugee survivors of sexual violence, and in the Korean American transnational anti-imperialist solidarity organizing space. In the course of her campaign, Hyejin connected with organizers in migrant justice and women's prisoner support, but discovered there was no centralized repository of strategy and analysis for survivor-defense campaigns in particular. She turned to INCITE! because of its presence in her education and because of her practical need for strategy and support in her campaign; it seemed like the only place that might offer resources. She cofounded Survived & Punished in the winter of that year.

———

Pilar Maschi grew up in the Lower East Side of Manhattan where she witnessed serious violence: addiction, displacement, and police murder. By the time she reached young adulthood, she was enraged. She began using drugs, squatting, prostituting, and eventually getting locked up. She worked with a reentry nonprofit to obtain her GED, and there met Ashanti Alston, an anarchist activist, speaker, writer, and former member of the Black Panther Party and Black Liberation Army. She felt familiar with anarchism from how it suffused the squatter and punk scenes and, through Alston, started meeting people in the revolutionary Black nationalist tradition, ultimately entering the networks that were beginning to form what would become Critical Resistance.

Pilar feels her "mission and purpose has been to fight not only with the working class but also with the underclass, those of us who are disregarded and forgotten." She takes great pride in having helped form what is now called abolition, and has enormous respect for the political prisoners and movement elders who taught her. She remembers feeling a sense of belonging when she first gave a presentation with Angela Davis present, having just recently been released. "She looked at me with such pride. I'll never forget, you know? And I was like, yeah, I want to be here. This is my home right here."

───

After a childhood in Miami and Central Florida, Kim Diehl went to a university in North Carolina. There, agitation against a plan to privatize campus service labor led her to an organization called Black Workers for Justice, a project of Black communists to organize rank-and-file workers in the South in the late '90s and early 2000s. Black Workers for Justice followed a strategy of worker-directed struggles for which they would provide leadership development. Kim got to "sit with them and be in the conversation to be in the planning." Over the next few years, she held various positions in movement spaces, from the Institute for Southern Studies to Southerners on New Ground, and received "very, very rigorous training" from the Service Employees International Union (SEIU), continuing to fight against privatization of public-sector employment. Around the year 2000, she was investigating privatized prison labor strategies emerging from the South when she encountered the Critical Resistance network.

Back then it was a very small "spiderweb" of people forming the network that became what it is now, before "funding and multiple layers of movement involvement." She describes it as being made up of people who had been incarcerated, those coming from Black nationalist organizing, the Malcolm X Grassroots Movement (MXGM), as well as charismatic figures like Rose Braz and Ruth Wilson Gilmore, whom Diehl looked up to with a mixture of romance and admiration, inspiring her to suck up "all of the knowledge and training of our movement." "I just follow the lead of folks and, you know, just did what folks asked of me," she says. Despite Critical Resistance being organized by chapter, she didn't take part in many local campaigns, instead relying on her experience in more professional movement settings to help craft its national structure behind the scenes.

Kim looks back on her formation in the labor movement as preparing her for her work at Critical Resistance in some ways, from her training to think in Maoist frameworks to the copwatch work coming from the MXGM, but ultimately the two movements "just didn't merge." They are still "different circles," she says. "Black trade-unionist threads are definitely not in circles looking at violence and alternatives to punishment." She sees this as a function of the diverging class character of the two movements. The movement around abolition "was either academic bourgeoisie and the lumpenproletariat—so people who were, you know, really on the margins, not able to work, underground—and Black trade unionists, working-class folks with jobs organizing in their shops and the public sector."

———

Stevie Wilson's political activity began early—growing up poor and Black in Boston, "some part of me has always been in a struggle," he writes, but being queer in the early '90s "made my struggle so much more public." This public struggle naturally turned to activism, and he became the vice president of a Boston queer youth alliance, through which he traveled and gave speeches "raising awareness regarding queer youth suicide and homelessness." He moved to Philadelphia for college, where he founded new queer activist organizations, participated in the ballroom scene, and was mentored by local activists Tyrone Smith and Hal Carter of Unity, Inc., a grassroots AIDS service organization founded by and for Black gay men.

Stevie situates himself in the transformative justice tradition as opposed to restorative justice, which he distinguishes as developing from communities of color and Indigenous people, respectively. For Stevie, "everyone has a part to play in the healing" in transformative justice. Centering the survivor and drawing the community into the healing process "is major for me." He sees this as a formalization of what he'd already been practicing in the ballroom scene, where people "could never rely upon the state to protect us or solve conflicts." Instead, the community helps people "get their needs met when the state abandons them."

———

Peter Hardie is a "sixty-five-year-old veteran of a lot of movements." He's been involved in organized socialist politics since the late '70s and is now sorting out his new role as an elder. He describes his entry into his own politics as taking part in struggles against South African apartheid, for African American and Chicano studies, and in the labor movement. His early "socialist home" was in the

Proletarian Unity League, a tendency coming out of the Students for a Democratic Society, which later became part of the Freedom Road Socialist Organization. Peter was equally involved in various Black radical formations, including a national network known as the Black United Front, the African Liberation Support Committee, and the Black Radical Congress. He worked in a factory for a decade and a half, then as staff for the SEIU in Boston, and then in South Africa as a coordinator for the AFL-CIO affiliate Solidarity Center.

———

Michelle Foy joined Fire By Night in the early 2000s. It emerged from an anarchist organization called Love and Rage, which had grown since 1989 from a North American newspaper to a federation. Love and Rage had dissolved in the late 1990s, and the Fire By Night Organizing Committee was the outcome of a decision by previous members to move toward revolutionary socialism and away from Marxism or anarchism in an attempt to "learn something new." Michelle never felt a particular affinity to anarchism but had been influenced by her teacher Ward Churchill's anti-Marxism, so the later adoption of Maoist practices along with ex–Love and Rage members required some political openness. Practically, this meant forming a cadre organization with intense study, commitment to political work, and collective organizing. Based in New York, Fire By Night worked with public-housing residents through the Eviction Defense Network and built a political-education initiative called Study and Struggle particularly aimed at activists coming out of the Hunter College Student Liberation Action Movement, which agitated around open admissions and affirmative action, in a continuation of '70s-era Third Worldist campus politics.

Michelle describes "missteps" and "mistakes" that some of the Fire By Night organizers made in relation to the Hunter struggle, and the guilt her collective felt over that was perhaps intensified by its all-white membership. It was in this context that Fire By Night was approached by people in Freedom Road about their organizations joining together. Despite already having engaged with communist formations, Michelle describes some trepidation at joining a Maoist organization: "I don't know if I'm ready for this," she recalls. The Freedom Road contingent they had joined had just undergone their own split, which meant she was thrust into some organizational processing that she didn't fully understand, though in time she came to appreciate the importance of the split.

The split had been triggered by a debate over an essay on the crisis of socialism, which catalyzed people's understanding of the need to come to terms with the failings of twentieth-century socialism "and not just say, oh, it's external problems," she explains. This crisis over the very idea of confronting internal political practices brought her much closer to the rest of the group, which she otherwise hadn't had much ideological affinity with. She gained more respect for Freedom Road and the way it and its predecessor organizations like the League of Revolutionary Struggle managed conflict and struggle.[1] "There were all kinds of internal contradictions and conflict and issues around power and leadership and people just not willing to question certain leaders or direction," she says, but this was now being worked through explicitly.

———

LV came up in an anarchist milieu of the early 2000s, a time of proliferating anarchist projects alongside and exceeding the antiwar and anti-globalization movements. There was a lot of "summit-hopping" and counter-convergence organizing during these years. Anarchists used the occasions of the Democratic and Republican parties' national conventions, such as the 2008 RNC in St. Paul and the DNC in Denver, to organize their own national-scale convergences. Within this antiauthoritarian network of mobilizations, LV notes that critiques of the consolidation of power were often dismissed. This shored up the influence and control of what LV's comrade called the "philosopher kings" of the movement, who counted among their ranks homophobes, transphobes, and abusers of (unremarked-on) power. The internal tensions of these mass movements were the crux from which Bash Back! emerged, first in Chicago and then across multiple US cities. LV names Bash Back! as one of two movements that are motivated to differentiate themselves from the radical spaces dominated by men. The other is the formation of feminist, survivor, and anti-rape groups that considered the power of collective rage and violence against countering sexual violence on a societal level and within the radical left. "We'll Show You Crazy Bitches" was a particularly paradigmatic 2010 communiqué. Recently, the Bash Back! network has been reanimated, LV notes, prompted again by threats to queer and trans life, and there are a number of convergences planned after a successful reunion in Chicago in the summer of 2023.

TRAJECTORY OF THE CONCEPT

Peter associates two different meanings of accountability with two different political periods of his life. One comes from his time as a member of a socialist organization, where it meant that your political practice was accountable to the people by following a political line determined by a collective decision-making process—effectively, it meant your commitment to democratic centralism, or adherence to political decisions voted on by the party. For the past decade or two, though, he's encountered it in a new register, where it now means something less party-political and more personal, like "trying to think about myself as a cis-heterosexual man. The privileges entailed in that, and my commitment to grappling" with them. He locates the origin of this latter meaning in his encounter in the 2000s with a robust queer and trans liberationist movement that made him realize his unconscious biases regarding "gender and patriarchy." This new terrain challenged him to interrogate how his political practice was inflected by male privilege, and he sees the valences of accountability as having been changed around the same time as this personal encounter.

In Esteban's telling, Philly Stands Up was at first strictly subordinate to Philly's Pissed, but as the work progressed tensions emerged when their understanding of accountability changed from serving as an arm for executing the demands of the survivors' group to taking in a growing understanding of community well-being. Through study, the Philly Stands Up group gained an understanding of transformative justice as somehow related to Indigenous practices of restoration, harmony, and repair. Decentering the impulse to punish revealed the interconnectedness of all relationships, which led them to recognize limits to accountability in people's material or social situations. Their work became a practice of creating a space for the perpetrator to simply begin communicating in a responsible way, to be vulnerable, because what they discovered was that such spaces were nowhere to be found. At this point their politics had evolved past being a subordinate affiliate of the survivors' group to something that had its own position, which was more committed to abolition and transformation of not only the perpetrator but their community. This is what grounds Esteban's understanding of accountability as a community practice somewhat restricted to providing a cluster of social support that can facilitate but cannot compel a personal and collective transformation.

For Pilar, abolition wasn't "sexy at all" when she began working with Critical Resistance, but it has become disturbed by changes in the movement she identifies as coming from class-privileged "carceral feminists" who learn abolition as a topic of academic study. The language has gone mainstream beyond what was dreamed of, but now she thinks the movement might need to take things more slowly and be more thoughtful. In her account, the movement for abolition has finally received widespread recognition in the wake of the George Floyd rebellions of 2020. This recognition was attained through a new, rapidly developed social media information mill that reduced core lessons and principles to phrases lacking important context. She sees accountability undergoing a similar process of conceptual degradation, but it is further torqued by a change in the makeup of the movement itself. Critical Resistance had always been "a multiculti, multigenerational, multi multi multi organization," but from the beginning, there had been a tension. She appreciated the coalition approach, but "who else is going to talk about inside the cage if not the people that have been inside the cage?" she asks. "As much as folks of color were in the movement, it was different. It was a class thing."

She feels accountable to her fellow "crimees," and thinks people talking about abolition need to use its language carefully because others look to them for leadership. For Pilar, abolition isn't vindictiveness, it's the fifty people who came with her when she turned herself in for a DV charge. Now, she worries that the movement has been "infiltrated" by people who "think that they're abolitionists because they were maybe drawn to it, but they haven't done the work" required to unlearn all the "conditioning that we've been subjected to."

Despite a marked humility in the movement's stance, which keeps even its fundamental principles general because they "recognize we don't have the answers," Pilar believes there are certain nonnegotiable commitments, like seeing yourself in the person who commits a bad act, not promoting incarceration, and centering the people who are most impacted by the prison-industrial complex. These were slowly formalized into a body of theory out of the experiences of people like her who had to struggle out of the clutches of the prison. Now the hoped-for mainstreaming has arrived, but with ambivalent effects: people without the context that produced its concepts can gain an inflated confidence through study, such that "vengeful" people misuse the painfully won fruits of the movement's organizing.

Both Hyejin and Emi see accountability as carrying a number of contradictory meanings. It has an abstract, aspirational meaning, like taking serious responsibility for harm, considering impact on others, and changing behavior. They also see it as having been stripped of meaning in the organizing communities they're in, misapplied or endowed with significance it can't provide. In these moments, invoking accountability can become a kind of apologism for inaction or lack of courage in responding to violence, or conversely, a veil over coercive demands for silence, punishment, etc. They note that people who aren't the survivor often project their own desires or values onto the term, turning "accountability" into a vehicle for their own internalized carceral or punitive logic.

Emi conjectures that INCITE! made a necessary disavowal of white-feminist or carceral approaches to sexual violence, but what that lost was an ability to discern or intervene in abuse dynamics, to support someone who's caused harm, etc. Because of this loss of specificity, people are now both too quick to apply technical terms like "abuse" to situations where it may not apply, and too reluctant to invoke it, because they only know it as a kind of social bludgeon. This ambiguity lets "people just sort of wring their hands and act like they don't know what to do and we can't figure it out," she says. "But the truth is that if you actually are trained to understand what to look for and how to assess the situation, it's a little bit easier. Like if abuse means something and it is a specific pattern of behavior that is identifiable by people who have the skills and knowledge and training to do that kind of identification, then it helps both the people who are concerned about the false accusations and the people who are surviving violence and abuse, because then we actually have an agreement about what it means."

Hyejin observes that tools for analyzing power have a reflexive quality, through which they can also structure power relations themselves. "These ideas, whether they're around gender justice or transformative justice or racial justice or prison abolition, all these things came from the need to identify and articulate power as it is now, and also to make an entrance into it," she puts it. For her that leads to the idea that the confusion of terms isn't simply a question of inattentive study or hasty popularization, but itself the sign of a struggle over the power to determine what transformative justice and abuse even are. There are different camps with different stakes in the terms having different meanings. As the abolitionist critique of the prison-industrial complex becomes more widespread, and more heterogeneous, people are joining the conversation and contesting the terms for their own use. This includes complex, multipart ideas like accountability or abuse that can require specialized training to apply accurately, as well as supposedly self-evident terms like *survivor*.

Stevie doesn't think that the movement is particularly skilled at dealing with conflict or practicing accountability. "Too often, groups break up because they didn't have procedures or processes," he explains, comparing this to "jumping off a cliff and trying to build your wings on the way down"—a variation on the sometimes positively invoked image of building a plane while flying it. "We have to practice conflict resolution before we need it." He relates this to criticism/self-criticism, which could be integrated into regular practice. He knows we have it in us to struggle with each other because we "are struggling against massive systems of oppression everyday."

For Peter, the vehicle for self-interrogation in the past would have been criticism/self-criticism, a practice typical of communist organizations like the Proletarian Unity League. While the idea was that this would promote members' growth and change, "the reality was that those spaces, those criticism/self-criticism spaces were very male, cis-hetero dominated," Peter says. He links the organizations' lack of openness to political dissent with their heterosocial order and sees that the movement's shift away from democratic centralism and dogmatism has made it more possible to work together through disagreement and toward an ecumenical search for truth, "whether it's in writings of Marx or it's in the writings of Cabral or it's in the writings of the Combahee River Collective." In this sense, accountability has almost diametrically changed in meaning: where forty years ago it meant a rigid adherence to a political line, now criticism will be focused on "how we treat each other as human beings."

This change to a less dogmatic practice of criticism as accountability has been positive, in his eyes. "I don't recall the last time some person was called on the carpet," Peter says. "I think we have been gentler with each other over the past few decades." He attributes that to the struggle of people who "aren't male and white," and is part of a men's study group to work through what he calls "counter-education" in order to be disciplined and work under the leadership of "non-men." On the one hand he sees this as a genuine question of organization and party functioning, but he seems to counterpose the focus on these "invisible cultural pushes" to what he sees as the proper object of self-criticism: systemic forces rather than people.

Michelle recalls how, when she served on a national leadership body of her organization, she had conversations about how older practices of criticism/self-criticism were intersecting with new training in Generative Somatics, a framework developed by "movement people" growing out of a Bay Area collective called Generation FIVE. Generation FIVE came to this framework in its transformative justice organizing to address the persistence of child sexual abuse. For Michelle, Generative Somatics captures people's "conditioned responses," which criticism/self-criticism can't account for—tendencies to respond to conflict by appeasing, or trying to fix it, or fleeing. The current reluctance on the left to offer criticism or feedback, a skill or ability that people can develop, also has much to do with an "overcorrection" after a period of extreme practices of criticism in the League of Revolutionary Struggle.

To her, the criticism then sounded destructive, like "people were kind of torn apart." At the same time, she is sensitive to the way that such practices were magnified in a kind of anticommunist game of telephone where all party organizing from the '70s and '80s could be reduced to one cruel struggle session. She counterposes this with a lesson she takes from Grace Lee Boggs in "Organization Means Commitment" about the need to reconcile yourself with some level of democratic centralism, but that it requires both terms. So the dysfunctional periods of harsh criticism sessions were an expression of a weakened emphasis on party democracy, which led to unquestioning cults of personality around leadership and extremely unhealthy dynamics. She sees this as continuing to have a negative influence even today, with the left "reaping the consequences" in terms of an attenuated capacity to share necessary criticism in political organizations.

The experiences of criticism/self-criticism are further away generationally and politically from the anarchist formations of the early 2000s that LV came up through. The trace of such is found though in the image of "struggle sessions," which are still linked associatively to the idea of accountability, along with a number of other present associations LV remarks on that were all decidedly negative. These include capitalist connotations of keeping accounts in order and criminal-justice connotations of punishment, as well as connotations within radical spaces that accountability is fraught with its perceived failures. As a concept or discourse it is also too general and unspecified, LV argues, to fully address the complexities of conflict. Conflict, on the interpersonal and societal scale, is complex and delicate. "*Accountability* is like a sledgehammer of a term," LV says, that doesn't always encapsulate the multiple nuances of a conflict and its ramifications.

In what is perhaps already an instance of a post-accountability practice within the re-emergent Bash Back! formation, "braver spaces" have been developed as one way of openly handling conflict: creating a no-holds-barred environment that does not reject violence. This is associated with the anarcho-insurrectionists and nihilists within Bash Back! Another framework that seemed more recent in its development is what LV counterposed directly to the term *accountability* as a "harm reduction" approach to conflict. These practices do not completely supplant what we might now call more "traditional" forms of accountability. LV refers to the Creative Interventions Toolkit as a resource over the past fifteen years to the present. Across these different orientations to handling conflict is a shared sense of its centrality to societal and interpersonal transformation. This interview being the most recent in this volume (conducted several years after the others), it is interesting to note that our project itself seems to share a reflective and desirous mood with those interested in reinvigorating Bash Back! Describing the Chicago convergence in 2023, LV says, "It felt like everybody was talking about how we deal with conflict and how conflict is navigated and theorizing about the different ways that people believe that conflict should be handled and should be dealt with."

CONCEPTUAL OPPOSITIONS

Compressing the breadth of the reflections shared with us into a short synthesis doesn't do justice to the rich texture of the interviewees' thinking. Still, in our analysis of the transcripts, we noticed certain common topics and difficulties that characterize the discussion of accountability and often recurred in seemingly opposed pairs or groups. This invalidates neither their assessment nor the concept itself, in our view, but points to the massive scope it is asked, and which it offers, to address. Some oppositions may represent tensions latent in the concept that complicate its application; others are surely the index of its fertility. We trace some of them here. They may helpfully serve as a guide through the interviews, though more insights are certainly there to be gleaned. As a preliminary outline of what we found from asking after the concept of accountability, these oppositions draw many of the varied contemporary uses and meanings together.

A traditional novelty
or a new tradition

Unsurprisingly for a project that aims to supplant the law, accountability and transformative justice draw some of their appeal from invoking a venerable lineage. Perhaps the most venerable of lineages in modernity: Indigeneity. Many of the interviewees mention that the ultimate source of the practices in question was Indigenous nations and their famed emphasis on repair and rejection of punishment. Another lineage that is often called on, with a similar but somewhat obscured relation to Indigeneity, is the Black radical tradition. We address some of the complexities of how this claim is deployed by non-Indigenous people in settler societies in the final essay. For now, we bring it up simply to note how it sits with the simultaneous recognition that what accountability aims to do is create something new—new modes of relating, a new society, even a new world.

This opposition is repeated on a smaller historical scale in the frequent claim that resolving conflict without the state is both what working-class communities of color have always done and something that needs the dedicated pedagogical effort of a movement to discover, elaborate, and generalize. That this resembles a contradiction is not, in our view, invalidating. In a society segregated by class and race, proletarian knowledge requires an organized effort to overcome its fractured, subordinate position and become a common understanding. And in the international division of labor that to this day menaces Indigenous societies with a genocidal incorporation as surplus, the overthrow of the present to bring about something globally new appears to be the only viable mode of survival. But the difficulty of thinking these two elements simultaneously seems to point to a deeper ambivalence about whether accountability overturns history—which is to say, the question of how it relates to revolution.

The organization of survivors
or the survival of the organization

One of the most inspiring but difficult elements of transformative justice is its analysis of punishment as part of a cycle of harm, not an end to it. Correctly identifying the supposed rehabilitative nature of prisons to be an alibi for their violent function in class rule demands a delicate approach, then, to alternative systems of addressing harm that aim to rehabilitate a perpetrator. This difficulty is surely what motivates what some of the interviewees call a punitive, "carceral" impulse behind some invocations of accountability. It can feel like "speaking another language," per Emi Kane, for survivors to say, "I don't want punishment. I actually care about this person. And I would like something to happen so that this cycle of harm is interrupted." Even within these movements, asking for accountability "gets so distorted and projected upon and turned into this ask for punishment."

You could imagine this to be a problem of the concept's uptake by people who haven't been fully acclimated to what realizing it would demand. But Esteban Kelly's experience tracked another dimension of this difficulty. He describes his group's evolution from a collective of men who were strictly responsible for carrying out a different group of survivors' demands into one that began to see the goal of repair as sometimes in conflict with what had been asked. This touches on a complicated dilemma: accountability only to survivors of harm may put the project of transformation at risk, while attending to larger questions of repair might alienate survivors and their supporters. Creating an accountable organization means establishing transparent processes for hearing concerns in advance of a conflict. Many times, too, organizations responding to an instance of harm will be composed of survivors, making it important to disentangle their feelings about their own past from the incident in front of them and what the survivor is requesting. All of this flows from the uncertain question: Who or what is the process for? The survivor, the organization—or the transformation?

Politics of accountability or accountability to a politics

The experiences that veterans of the Maoist parties share of their encounters with criticism/self-criticism paint it as a dynamic vehicle for analysis of political activity aimed at self-improvement, while conceding that its notoriously grim reputation has some basis in fact. But since the '90s, they describe a different political landscape, where accountability is much more likely to be an occasion for reflection on personal conduct. This has left the organizations in better shape emotionally but may have kept them away from more volatile political engagement out of an atrophied capacity for productive disagreement. On the other hand, the transformative justice practitioners more often mention coming to articulate their politics in an explicit way after already organizing around concrete campaigns or projects. Here the politics of accountability develop precisely in the absence of abstract commitments to a program or line, which allows it to pursue real developments in the political configuration of the world, but might become paralyzed when contradictory demands—like a survivor's wish for punishment, for example—conflict with the goal of abolition. For LV, who came up in anarchist scenes and pursues accountability as a dialogic social process, accountability is about a revolutionary "commitment to dialogue with yourself and with your comrades and sitting with [conflict] and working through that." For the more insurrectionary and nihilistic tendencies within Bash Back!, the politics of accountability are somewhat irrelevant to the desire to amplify antagonisms, not necessarily with the hope or will for resolution.

For Hyejin Shim, working with incarcerated survivors gives accountability another, pressing meaning: a mode of equitably relating to the person they are advocating for when the relationship is premised on their captivity. This informs answers to highly consequential questions for her: How do you tell the person's story in the way they want it told, while pushing back on elements that are unstrategic or even harmful? Accountability here seems to name the subordination of individual responses to a larger political goal. Kim Diehl describes her experience working through this as a process of "principled compromise," which, of course, requires some agreed-upon principles. Keeping these principles in sight helped Critical Resistance navigate what might otherwise have been fatal conflicts. Sometimes the outcome was an undesirable one: a closed chapter, for example, but for the good of the organization's longevity. Yet for the transformative justice movement, discovering what those principles might be seems to have been facilitated by precisely this freedom from foregone political commitments. This returns us to the question of how the traditions the movement is working in determine its capacity for discovering something new.

Generalized adoption
or adoption of generality

Related to this question is a tension in how the body of knowledge circulates. All of the professional transformative justice practitioners share feelings of ambivalence about the ways their hard-won understandings of accountability have been taken up by an enthusiastic public that may not share the context for how they were developed or meant to be applied. Pilar Maschi goes so far as to say that someone who only comes to transformative justice through study—that is, without the direct experience of criminalization or harm that it was formed to combat—won't know what to do with it in a conflict. The concept's widespread adoption has led to serious enough misuse that Pilar wonders whether this was the right strategy: "The movement has changed. So now I'm trying to grab a hold of it and bring it back just a little bit, just a notch."

This disappointment is a sign not only of the risk that the critical, challenging thrust of the concept could be lost in its popularization, but that the theory of how to change society by sharing this knowledge—a notable, and admirable, dimension of the movement is its commitment to popular education—might need more specification. If the concept can be so maimed in its use by people without the necessary experience, how should it teach the people it needs to teach without losing its meaning in the process? This goes for movement specialists too: Emi's own experience as a survivor going through an accountability process after years of facilitating them challenged much of what she thought she knew. This has further implications for the theory of coalition or conspiracy between people with different levels of exposure to the carceral state collaborating to overcome it. The missteps they mention underscore the weight of the commitment to centering the people most impacted by the prison system. Doing this with proper care might impose a real limit on the movement's spread outside of it, but without attaining some level of popular support, social transformation is impossible.

For LV, the widespread adoption of any one accountability practice in particular is less important than devising practices in prolonged and expansive dialogues with communities, revolutionary spaces, radical formations, etc. This is framed as the necessary work of addressing conflict. In fact, LV describes this need as parallel to the infrastructural and basic demands of creating any viable collective. "At this point, every collective that I enter into, every movement space that I enter into, I try to tell people we need to approach conflict in the same way that we approach food or feeding massive groups of people."

Class fractions
or fracturing of the class

This leads us to the final opposition in which all others are refracted: the class character of the movement. Pilar offers one pole: she understands herself to be accountable to her "fellow crimees," expressed here not primarily as accountability to survivors as such, nor women, nor the community, nor the left, and so on. Tracing the history of the movement as it came to assume its organizational form illuminated how responding to this tension gave it its current structure. Stevie Wilson pithily captures the situation facing organizers in Black working-class communities: "We had to make something from nothing while being told we ain't shit!" Other practitioners describe the early abolitionist scene in similar terms, coalescing slowly out of prison reentry programs and punk music scenes until a semi-professionalized layer could gain enough of a foothold in academia and nonprofit organizations to secure larger grants and more funding. These professionalizing advocates turned the small network into a career-sustaining infrastructure. Even those outside of those semi-professionalized layers may be in conversation with the methods they devise, an overlap illustrated by the circulation of the Creative Interventions Toolkit in radical anarchist circles and indeed spaces that refuse or resist formalization.

Kim Diehl observes that the Black trade-unionist circles that trained her politically didn't overlap with the abolitionists. She puts this down to its character as an academic or bourgeois-lumpen coalition, as opposed to "folks with jobs organizing in their shops and the public sector." She herself embodies the movement's attempt to straddle this divide, seeing her role as a "co-conspirator" to people like her brother, who had done time in prison. In a similar key, Peter Hardie appraises the nonparty movements as drawing from "new knowledge" not based on the literature of the revolutions nor the communist tradition but "the real-life experiences of people who decided that they are tired of oppression." This encounter has reciprocally enriched the communist formations, but he sees its lack of familiarity with this literature as a failing on the part of the communist organizations to meet these newer organic projects where they're at.

All of these interviewees describe a similar situation—one of organized working-class militancy increasingly reduced in size and potency, and at a distance from a new coalition of the fractions of a disorganized working class held together by meager access to bourgeois patronage, all the while subject to the ever-louder drone of predation by the prison system. This is, in effect, the situation mapped most decisively by Critical Resistance cofounder Ruth Wilson Gilmore in her 2007 *Golden Gulag*, which traces the massive, rapid expansion of the prison-industrial complex in California to the stalling out in the 1970s of the model of growth that, for much of the century, had seemed to project the steady incorporation of waged workers into the industrial production process far into the future. This model had also formed the premise for most revolutionary organizing against it but encountered a crisis of profitability around the same period as the historic, time-cracking revolts, leaving the state with idle excess capacity and workers the capitalists had to shake off their balance sheets. While there was a deliberate capitalist-class project to shatter the social bases of proletarian militancy, profit imperatives, too, weighed on the possible paths out of this moment of crisis for the capitalist state. The outcome was the transformation from a society with a mass industrial proletariat to the more class-polarized, prison-industrial society that abolitionists diagnose as the salient form of capitalist misery today.

Working after the failure of the global revolts of the '70s to cohere into a systemic challenge, Gilmore and others attended to the political decomposition of the working class by following it where the state had dispersed it: out of the point of industrial production and into the "hell factories in the field," as a pivotal article by Mike Davis on prison construction puts it. The seeming disappearance of the collective agent of change, which the parties all had hoped to organize, took with it the horizon of revolution. One sign of this dispersal came in a previous interview we conducted with Stevie Wilson.[2] Discussing the difficulties organizing fellow prisoners, he notes that "growing up, they don't feel a part of their community. They don't feel a part of their neighborhood. You see that a lot of them don't feel part of their family. And then you come to prison stuff, let's talk about community. They're looking at you like, 'What? What "community?"'"[3]

In the organizing that became transformative justice, a dimension of the occluded revolutionary horizon had been preserved after its disappearance in the '80s counterinsurgency, the trace of which can be seen in the now common use of *abolition* to describe the aspiration for what in the past may have gone under the name of *communism*. It was this sensitive attention to the concrete location and composition of the class that allowed the abolitionist movement to anticipate the form in which generalized revolt would return, almost fifty years later. But as the interviewees lament, anticipation does not on its own unify the scattered class into a self-acting political force. As a contemporary descendant of "survival pending revolution," accountability practices offer many deep gifts, not least of which is the capacity to proceed, caringly and inventively, from failure. Reflecting on their own understandings of its failures, the following interviews may contain the seeds of whatever productive failures we can hope to discover next.

1
Following their 1999 split, both factions kept the name Freedom Road Socialist Organization. Peter and Michelle were both members of the tendency that later changed their name in April 2019 to Liberation Road.

2
Stevie Wilson, "Inside Agitator," *Pinko*, no. 2, July 2020, https://pinko.online/pinko-2/inside-agitator.

3
We take up this quote as the title of our collective's reflective essay that closes this volume.

AFTER ACCOUNTABILIT

Pilar
Maschi

Pilar Maschi came to abolition and transformative
justice through a prison-sponsored treatment
program. After becoming pregnant while
incarcerated, Pilar joined a reentry program
that put her in touch with the networks that were
beginning to form what became Critical Resistance.
She was brought into the organization and hired
as staff, initially to organize former prisoners,
including those from her old program. Pilar has
now been organizing against the prison-industrial
complex for over twenty years.

ADDISON VAWTERS

Hi, Pilar! Thank you for joining me today. We're conducting
these interviews with people from different movements to
learn about their personal history with, and introduction to, the
concept of accountability. And then we'll get at some of those
questions in between and see what emerges.

PILAR MASCHI

That is very exciting, Addison! Accountability, like community,
has become a popular word in our organizing spaces. So, I'm
happy that Pinko is centering accountability in the abolitionist
movement. It's been exciting and challenging to experience the
abolition movement becoming popular in mainstream society.
In the past few years, I have experienced newer formations of
organizers collectively having a difficult time committing to
anti-authoritarian and nonpunitive principles and practices. Our
prison-industrial complex abolitionist history, which contains
our principles and practices, needs to be widely accessible and
shared throughout abolitionist spaces.

AV

Could you start by describing a timeline of your political
development starting from when you first felt radicalized? That
can serve as a framework for the conversation.

PM

I am a queer Latina of many different heritages. I was born
and raised in New York City, mostly in NYC projects, a.k.a.
NYC public housing in the Upper West Side and in other
neighborhoods like Washington Heights and Chelsea. I also
lived in Miami and Puerto Rico, and in my teens to late twenties
in Alphabet City, the Lower East Side, Soho, Fort Greene,
and Williamsburg in Brooklyn, and Hell's Kitchen and West
Harlem became home.

One of my first rebellious instincts came out when I was
about eleven years old. It was 1982, during a time when me and
my Upper West Side communities had been invaded by real
estate developers. I remember a tall high-rise building being
built in my apartment's kitchen window view. There were
other high-rises rapidly rising up, and the construction of this
particular one was tearing up one of the last remaining lots

and erasing this green space that our community used all year round—so much history of love and happiness now vanished. Before the building construction every winter, this green space would light up with Christmas lights and pine trees. It became a wondrous place. Much of Manhattan would purchase their Christmas trees there. It was also a place occupied by a yearly carnival and the families in our neighborhood loved it. We had gardens and parks all around us.

At the same time, the drugs had arrived, my block was on fire, friends my age had jobs now and were making cash. Mis tias y tios who I grew up with were now getting hooked on crack and literally disappearing. I understood then and there the connections between real estate development and violent urban displacement. It's through this violent displacement that developers would use the pouring of drugs into our communities for their benefit, and an increase in broken windows policing was the answer to the New York City government's "tough on crime" political framing and supposed "quality of life crimes." The cops were doing daily sweeps; it was always hunting season in our hoods. This led to mass house police raids, which led to arrests and evictions, which led to incarceration and houselessness, which led to the warehousing and death of our people and a successful re-colonization of a neighborhood.

As I became older and became a witness and survivor of the same harm that I saw my tios and tias in my hood go through here, I was displaced, migrating into the next neighborhood. I experienced this formula over and over again. It was the same circumstances of massive neglect, exploitation, and starvation of resources stolen from a particular community. I knew someone was benefiting, and it wasn't us. I knew this was rooted in racism, it was punitive thinking and behavior against those of us in the margins. Nonetheless, it was complicated, because with all of that pain and despair was resistance and freedom. It was a very creative and exciting time.

When I was sixteen years old, my father was murdered; he was shot multiple times at close range with a nine millimeter, murdered by an off-duty NYPD officer. From a young age I was extremely aware of my surroundings and what was happening to me, my family, and my community, and not knowing how to cope with all of this trauma, I journeyed through drug addiction and other harm. So far, I have survived. In fact, I was able to experience the purest form of love through the birth of my baby, Autumn.

After being incarcerated while pregnant during one of my skid bids on Rikers Island, in the Rose M. Singer women's jail, which some of us called Rosie's, I was released to a substance abuse residential treatment program and was able to have my baby unshackled. I was court mandated to this treatment facility for two years. I used this time to really work on myself and raise Autumn. I benefited greatly from both therapy and the twelve step program, and at the same time, I had issues with some of the twelve step program's concepts. Although I didn't know it at the time, this process of critical thinking around my treatment and the use of cognitive therapy and the twelve step program helped me in developing my analysis of abolition and the prison-industrial complex.

While still in treatment, I went into the Fortune Society voluntarily to help myself take my GED. There I would meet Ashanti Alston, who was a former Black Panther and an anarchist. Through him I learned about abolition and began to meet our radical elders. I was introduced to the movements of the Black Liberation Army (BLA), the Black Panthers, the Zapatistas, Los Macheteros, MOVE, the Young Lords, and beyond. In 2000–2001, while I was still in the Fortune Society, Ashanti and a few other staffers who worked in the Education department and were my tutors were also part of the group organizing the Critical Resistance Northeast Regional Conference. This was my introduction to Critical Resistance and abolition.

In 1998, while I was on the run, over three thousand folks attended the first Critical Resistance conference—Beyond the Prison Industrial Complex. I was unable to make that conference.

The Fortune Society was a key catalyst to my growth, connecting me to abolitionists such as Ashanti, Eric Appleton, Rachel Herzing, Shana Agid, Ashley Hunt, and others. I'm lucky they took me under their wings, as this led to me interning with the Critical Resistance New York City (CRNYC) chapter and leading an outreach project. I was participating in many if not all of the CRNYC working groups our chapter had been creating. I was also participating in CR National working groups. I was home and I was safe. And this all made sense to me. I couldn't fully accept Narcotics Anonymous, and, since that realization, there was urgency for me in sharing how much resistance and abolition was necessary! Recovery goes beyond substance abuse. Self-determination and collective liberation is our power.

Our chapter recognized that people most harmed by the prison-industrial complex needed to be represented in our movement spaces and the organization and chapter was supportive of that, so we did something about it. Eric Appleton and I created a popular education curriculum outreach project called La Casita Project to bring in women and their children from the La Casita Program, the residential substance abuse treatment program in the South Bronx that I was residing in at the time with my baby, Autumn. Once the La Casita Program gained attention and commitment by more Critical Resistance NYC chapter members, comrades Alex Reitzes, Liz Bishop, Jonathan Wilson, and Lailan Huen co-led the project and helped us evolve La Casita Project into four subprojects, and at this capacity, the La Casita Project lived for ten years. The La Casita Project became a model for other CR local chapter projects like the Chrysalis Project of the CR Gainesville chapter and A New Way of Life from the CR Los Angeles Chapter. Critical Resistance grew to having eleven chapters at one point, and I became a national staffer that supported chapters in bringing people most impacted into our movement. I was first hired as the Former Prisoner and Family Outreach Coordinator in 2003, and this grew into the Membership and Leadership Development Director, until I left my CR staff position in 2011.

In 2005, a comrade—Lisa Ortega from the group Rights for Imprisoned People with Psychiatric Disabilities—learned that a new jail was being proposed in the South Bronx, ten blocks away from where the La Casita Residential Program was, a few blocks from where the CR office was, and where I lived raising Autumn. The NYC Mayor Mike Bloomberg and Department of Corrections Commissioner Martin Horn were leading a reformist move to build a 2,040-bed jail for mothers with a baby nursery in it, under the guise of overcrowding at Rikers Island, neglectful conditions inside Rikers, and the proposed jail location being in a neighborhood that made the cage closer to family members. We quickly helped form the coalition Community in Unity with several other groups in the Bronx and led the first No New Jails campaign in NYC, which our coalition ultimately fought from 2005 and won in 2009!

My mission and purpose has been to fight not only with the working class but also with the underclass, those of us who are disregarded and forgotten. I've been organizing to abolish the prison-industrial complex for twenty-plus years and am grateful to have directly helped shape this movement. I never thought the movement for prison-industrial complex abolition would reach the heights it's achieved in recent years, or that strategies like defunding the police would be almost considered mainstream. I think there is a ton of room for the concept of defunding the police, and TJ, for instance, to evolve, but there are aspects of the prison-industrial complex like abolition and TJ that we fundamentally must honor. We cannot compromise on them.

AV

Thank you Pilar, this has already been so insightful. Can you speak more on Critical Resistance?

PM

I see the prison-industrial complex abolition movement somewhat beginning with groups and individuals who came together around the publication of the book *Instead of Prisons* and with the birth of Critical Resistance and other allied organizations. I see it also coming from our elders and past movements in fragments, perhaps. Though there weren't many of us being as explicitly PIC abolitionists as the group Justice Now and Critical Resistance were. Justice Now was cofounded by Critical Resistance family Cassandra Shaylor and Cynthia Chandler and we all worked closely supporting each other's work. Justice Now worked with women in prison. There were PIC abolition core movement builders who were doing their thing fighting for PIC abolition in other formations. In Critical Resistance, Rachel Herzing was my direct supervisor and mentor. Kai Lumumba Barrow and Ashanti Alston were my coworkers in NYC. We were representing the Northeast region and we worked in the Brooklyn office. Our NYC office moved throughout the years from Harlem in 2000, to Brooklyn in 2003, Manhattan in 2005, and then to a storefront in the South Bronx from 2006 to 2011. Rose Braz and Rachel Herzing worked in the Bay. Throughout the years, we've had several staffers working in CR offices. When I began working for CR, Ellen Barry, Dorsey Nunn, Linda Evans, Claude Marks, and Linda Thurston were my Advisory Committee Board. I was absolutely captivated and [at] home. And there was such a commitment to our political prisoners and political elders. I had immense respect for the people who were our leaders, the ones who taught us, you know? Black nationalism, the campaign to free Mumia. I was just embracing all of it and wanted to learn all of it. And I wanted other people who were down, who I had gone to treatment with or lived on the streets with. To me accountability was about bringing our people into these spaces. I also saw resistance as a part of recovery. Though I have learned from Narcotics Anonymous, I could not get 100 percent down with NA. It wasn't my thing. But organizing was. Fighting was. And transforming my anger was. That was what I was like. We are evolving, I'm growing, and I was just all about that.

AV

Can you say more about the makeup of Critical Resistance?

PM

We're a multicultural, multigenerational, multiclass, and multi-multi organization. I'm sure people in the room dealt with addiction, but quietly. But they weren't the people that I survived with. They weren't the women that were in the program. And many folks had learned about abolition through study. There weren't many people who had learned abolition through forced struggle. And it was tough at times to have members center this. We committed to prioritizing the people who are most impacted by the PIC in our chapters and in our chapter work, and so my role early on became helping people figure out how to do that, and helping members get to a place where they wanted to do that.

This is my home right here, because I was unconditionally accepted. I want to say that again. I was accepted unconditionally. Now, though, I don't think we should necessarily be accepted unconditionally. Well, I guess it's complicated. I think language can be a vital tool which can be both harmful and positive for abolition. And getting back to the fundamentals: when we talk about accountability, if somebody invests and commits to being an abolitionist, they're going to have to unlearn all the conditioning that we've been subjected to. Things that we don't even notice we do that counter abolition. We have to dismantle the prison-industrial complex in our head. Today there is bashing, humiliating, punishing, and seeking revenge on your comrades and intimate partners online; back in the day we didn't relate to each other like this. I'm not saying I'm excusing people's behaviors. I am saying I should be able to support some if not all parties involved in an interpersonal conflict. People should be able to inquire, question, and even support anyone in any circumstance, even community members who have harmed within our community. That is abolition. In movements, some of us assume and cast judgment while using the term "survivor" loosely, as mainstream society has. Many of us are survivors of the prison-industrial complex and survivors of other harm and that needs to be factored into the identities of the "survivor." I'm not sure I identify with or use "survivor" anymore, as there's many assumptions and threats behind the term.

It's important that we listen to each other, that we become aware of the words and phrases that are carceral and harmful. We have been so accustomed and conditioned to use these terms, we don't realize we are causing harm.

There has been an incredible amount of social media accusation, public shaming . . . literally cop-calling. I don't support that behavior, this social media cop-calling. Because that's what that is when you accuse someone of harm and publicly state crimes allegedly committed by your community member online, you're basically filing an online police report.

I have a difficult time trusting people in these spaces. Some of us who may actually mean well may actually be gatekeeping community spaces, taking ownership of something that isn't actually ours. I think this happens often with POC community spaces.

AV

We've been wondering if the Maoist practice of criticism/self-criticism had any influence in the formation and evolution of transformative justice or accountability?

We were originally trying to work out a way to recognize that conflict happens and that if we wanted to abolish the PIC, we needed a way to deal with our problems on our terms, in a way that was nurturing, loving, caring, not based in punishment, and certainly not based in revenge. This has to come from love. As Che Guevara said, "The true revolutionary is guided by great feelings of love." We wanted to develop a way of addressing harm that was also fair and transparent. Where everyone impacted has a say in their future, in the decisions that come out of a transformative justice process. Some people were really interested in that and took it on. They created organizations around that, like Creative Interventions [Oakland, CA]. Rachel and Isaac at Creative Interventions published a 600-page toolkit, and I think it's great, it's very useful. It was based on communities that dealt with interpersonal violence situations within their communities. They established language around what a witness is, what a bystander is, they break it down. And I constantly offer those tools to new people who are organizing. I tried to use the toolkit with the No New Jails collective, encouraging newer organizers to learn about Critical Resistance's concept of accountability.

Using the toolkit didn't go as planned, and things didn't really work out, which is also an important lesson. The tools of transformative justice are far from perfect. You need to be able to trust one another though in political work. And it gets messy. People sleep with each other, you know? People of all genders and sexualities. Queers are not immune to cop behavior. My ex, a self-proclaimed abolitionist, called the cops on me. Really disturbing. Luckily I had a lot of support. My communities came to support me in the process and court. Michelle, your coeditor, actually helped me a lot during that time. I ended up somehow turning myself in when I wanted to with my attorney, which was a first for me, and I had mad people backing me up. That's accountability. That is something I've never seen in my life. Anytime I have been locked up before in the past, nobody came.

Do you remember what happened at *Commune Magazine*?

AV

I do.

PM

I was just like, "How is this happening? How are they actually shutting down a formation like this, without a process?" It's like, that is exactly what I'm talking about. I keep saying I feel like we're being infiltrated by some serious, hardcore, carceral feminist theory. Why did people join abolition? They were perhaps drawn to it, but they need to still do the work. So the way that they respond and react is punitive. The fundamentals of abolition are sometimes intentionally general because well, we are still envisioning what abolition is. We don't have the answer, number one. We recognize that we don't have all of the answers. We're still figuring it out. I think what's happening right now is that carceral feminism is interfering in our spaces, and that's just the term I'm applying maybe incorrectly. It's terrible, it's like you want the worst outcome for the individual. You don't want the best. You don't want the good. That is definitely not what abolition is. Abolition is simple. I raised my daughter as an abolitionist, so I definitely can talk about it in really simple and practical ways. There are no bad people, people do bad things. You know what I mean?

AV

Yes.

PM

We recognize that. We need to see ourselves in opportunities for solutions for peace, repair, and resolve, for every person involved, harmed, and harmful in some circumstances, everyone who is incarcerated, every person who commits an act, a horrendous act. I think that what's happening right now is a type of bullying. I couldn't believe how shut down I felt during said conflicts and fallouts. I was being pressed to feel a certain way. I had to be on the side of the women and if I wasn't on the side of the quote unquote "victims," the survivors, then I was violent, as violent as whoever they thought the person that allegedly committed the harm was. Moreover, why is it shocking to other people that we lie? As humans we all lie. You don't have a responsibility to trust women only, you have a responsibility to make your own inquiry. Find out for yourself what happened, through mediation perhaps, and the TJ process.

Both the No New Jails conflict and the *Commune* conflict were huge lessons. I would love to revisit them to learn. Abolition is about getting rid of the criminal justice system and creating new systems in its place, and some of us may be struggling to live up to that. We need to learn more how to bring compassion and understanding into our spaces, which is why I appreciate you all undertaking this exploration.

AV

We have all observed or been a part of failed attempts at accountability, which is what spurred this project. Earlier you mentioned that we were unsure how you felt about the unconditional acceptance of those who commit harm. Can you speak more on that?

PM

Sure. When I was in my reentry program, I spent several years in cognitive behavioral therapy (CBT). In CBT you're taught to assimilate back into society by taking personal responsibility for your addiction, as though that will help you stay "clean." I find so much recovery language, such as the term "clean," and the framework to be harmful and problematic. CBT is obviously very helpful for some people, and I don't actually want to say that it doesn't work at all, but it is punitive. I think the term "love unconditionally" actually points us towards forgiveness. I know a couple of abolitionists who are amazing and I love them so much, and they're the first people to tell me they don't forgive. Abolition isn't necessarily about forgiveness. True. Though how else do we find peace? I don't know. I was raped several times, some of them I forgive. We have to at least be open to forgiving. And I'm open to forgiving even my worst enemy. I am.

So abolition is about repair and minimizing the harm in a way that is not promoting incarceration. If you're over here rooting to lock someone up, whether he's a cop or not, and then calling yourself an abolitionist in the same breath, I just don't think that's reasonable. I don't think that sends out a clear message about what abolition is. Because when we promote someone's incarceration, even a police officer's, we are promoting the incarceration of our people, of the person that we love the most, ourself and our family and our loved ones. We're saying that it's OK. We legitimize the prison-industrial complex. And who is it that gets impacted by that, whether it's a hate crime, or not . . . Whatever gets invented and created, it is another reason to lock somebody up—it could be meant for a KKK member—but who has to pay the price? Always our people, always poor people, people of color, Black people. So what are we really doing? I'm often the annoying person that's like, "I'll say something. I can't keep my mouth shut. I'll say something." If I see somebody doing it, old school abolitionists or the new school, I'll say something that's hopefully not harsh, but very direct. I will say something because I have to.

I have been put in really bad positions, like my ex putting a warrant out on me, getting me locked up. I could have pressed charges in retaliation and it could have gone back and forth, and because I'm somebody of principle, I did not do that.

AV

What are some of the methods used by the abolitionist movement?

PM

I think in some spaces we are moving the classroom to the organization—everything is training now. Another training, another cohort, and another pod, all these buzzwords. I know we had to make do during the pandemic, but before the pandemic, we were all about different forms of popular education that involved communities on the ground, and right now, I don't experience most spaces tapping into that. I don't want to be negative, and there are groups that are trying. Our mutual aid projects are vast. And I do appreciate the groups that are trying to penetrate prisons and figure out how to organize with prisoners. I see more of that than former prisoner support and leadership. I don't see a lot of people thinking about how to bring former prisoners into current abolitionist movement work, and this is not OK. Every single formation should be working on this as an ongoing priority. Our movements can always do more mutual aid. We need to end pretrial detention on a mass scale. Critical Resistance's Stop Urban Shield campaign out West has been absolutely badass. CR is definitely strong in leading anti-policing, anti-militarization campaigns.

And there are a lot of small autonomous collectives of different formations that I really, really love that are not getting the support they need and are working regardless. Nonprofits are collecting all the big philanthropy money. Thankfully Critical Resistance has figured out a way to raise money from within the communities that are involved, from donors, academic, and activist worlds.

I'm still alive. I'm still breathing. While my other peers, my other comrades, my other crimees, many of them are not alive, many of them are locked up. I'll always know that that's who I am first accountable to. I will continue to be guided by great feelings of love for our elders and ancestors who came before me. The movement has changed in many directions and so now I'm trying to grab a hold of it and bring it back just a little bit.

AV

I love that.

PM

Thank you. All right, hon.

AV

Thank you. Good night.

Michelle Foy

Michelle Foy is a white woman in her forties
and a longtime socialist organizer who has been
active in Freedom Road (now Liberation Road) for
more than two decades. She works as a finance
and administration director for a nonprofit
association, and began her career with socialism
with a political formation called Fire By Night,
which emerged after an anarchist organization
called Love and Rage dissolved in the late 1990s.

LOU CORNUM

It can be a pretty open-ended conversation, but I'd be curious just to hear about your experience with different organizations like Fire By Night, after your experience with Freedom Road, or was that before?

MICHELLE FOY

It was before. Fire By Night started in 1999 after Love and Rage dissolved.

LC

Is Love and Rage [related to] Freedom Road?

MF

Fire By Night was a very small group of folks in New York and in the Bay Area. I actually was never in Love and Rage. I tried to join and they were like, "We're falling apart," you know, "now's not the time." It was basically out of the dissolution of Love and Rage that folks were like, "Let's come back together and see if we want to learn something new," with this specific idea, the likelihood, of moving towards revolutionary socialism and Marxism and away from anarchism. So we formed in 1999. It seems like such a short-lived thing, I think it was only a year, but it was a very intense year; we were engaged in pretty rigorous study and collective organizing. We were doing work around housing and displacement, and specifically working with public housing residents through the Eviction Defense Network here in the Bay Area. And then, there's organization-building, building a cadre organization from the ground up and all that that entails, which you're obviously familiar with. So, it felt like I went through a really involved process with Fire By Night. It was really important for my political development to be a part of that. And it was also really difficult when the folks in New York said that they no longer wanted to build the organization. We were in the process of establishing this project called Study and Struggle, which is a political education kind of cadre or school for developing folks, particularly coming out of the Hunter College struggle in New York.

LC

Sort of like a Freedom School idea.

MF

Exactly. In terms of the plan for Study and Struggle, we were going to bring in political practice to it as well. There were some missteps, mistakes that our folks—the Fire By Night folks—made in relationship to the Hunter College organizing. Some of the folks at Hunter were angry and raised their concerns with the Fire By Night members in New York . . . It was just like, "We fucked up," and they were like, "Yeah, we fucked up," and there was a good bit of shame that arose from that experience, from what I observed. So we're just going to throw in the towel. And at that point, we were an entirely white organization. So that contradiction was really critical in relationship to the New York organizing. Those of us here in the Bay Area, we sort of remained together as a very small collective. There were five or six of us at that point, and that's when Freedom Road came to us. We had done some joint studies and had been to some of their events, and had done organizing against Prop 21, which was the youth criminalization initiative here in California. We were on really good comradely terms with folks. So they invited us to a study and said, "What do you all think about considering joining?"—basically merging or coming into Freedom Road? So that's what we did. And I was like, "A Maoist organization?" I don't know if I'm ready for this, if that's how it's identified.

LC

Is that how they presented themselves? Did they make a pitch, or was it just like, "You kind of have the same orientation, why don't we team up?"

MF

Yeah. And I think it was like, OK, we come out of the New Communist Movement and we study Mao and Mass Line. I think some members probably would uphold that the organization is Maoist, although far fewer today than in 2000. This was just a year or so following the split that happened in Freedom Road.

LC

Yeah. So it was the Midwest contingent that was more sort
of Stalinist.

MF

Yeah, exactly. So we kind of came in at the tail end of that.
People were recovering from that process, which was tough and
emotional for all involved.

LC

Wow, what a time to enter.

MF

It was very interesting. We didn't experience any of it; we didn't
know any of those folks in the other Freedom Road. So, now,
twenty-one years later, we're in Liberation Road, and…did you
know we changed the name?

LC

Yes, that was kind of confusing to me at first. There were two
Freedom Roads, but now there's a Liberation Road. I think
that's the line.

MF

It was like, "We just have to do it," in terms of the name change.
They're not going to do it. And it's way too confusing to have
two organizations with the same name. We tried three different
times to change our name, there was some resistance and it was
tough, emotional for some to let go of our name.

LC

What was it like coming in during that post-break time? Was
there a lot of conversation within the organization about it?
Was it something that was being processed openly, or was it
something that had already been there? Do you feel like you
kind of entered after the processing?

MF

I think there was still a lot of processing. I think I didn't totally
understand it, or was not fully clued into it. Not having gone
through it, I just kind of felt naive about it all. It was like, "OK, so
this is history," or, "This just happened, I don't really understand

what it all means, except I'm glad I'm with these folks instead of the others." I certainly feel like I wouldn't be aligned with the other folks. There was definitely some processing, and I think in some ways it really just consolidated our politics that much more. You know the piece that contributed to this split on the crisis of socialism? I mean, obviously, it's just one written piece, it doesn't represent everything about the split, but it really crystalized the political differences between the two different camps. It brought people that much closer to this idea of like, "Oh, we really need to reconcile and come to terms with the failings of twentieth-century socialism," and not just say, "Oh, it's external problems."

LC

To really look at what internal failures we're always kind of ascribing to external forces.

MF

Right. So that just kind of allowed us to dig into it more deeply. And talking about this question of organizational summations or self-reflection, thinking about some of our predecessor groups, like the League of Revolutionary Struggle (LRS), some of the people that came out of that really being like, "Let's look at this more closely." There was a lot that was really great and hugely impactful about the work that LRS did. And there were all kinds of internal contradictions and conflicts—issues around power and leadership and people not willing to question certain leaders or directions. So all of that I found really interesting. And again, not having been in LRS and not being of that generation, there's so much to learn there. Some of the former LRS folks are actually still in the process of summing up the experience; they are planning to put out a book, which will be great. So much to draw from that.

LC

Was there ever any further communication with the other Freedom Road?

MF

I mean, certainly there were still relationships.

LC

Persistent relationships, that's what's so interesting. It's like,
you break up, but you can never really stop being in relation.

MF

Yeah, exactly. It's like co-parenting almost [*laughs*]. So it sounds
like some people definitely stayed in touch with folks, and then
they got hit with the FBI raid.

LC

I didn't know that.

MF

Yeah, they were. What year would that have been . . . the
late aughts, like 2009, 2010. I was on the National Executive
Committee then, and I remember talking about it, like, "Isn't it
interesting that we have the same name as them and yet none of
our members got visits by the FBI," like the FBI understood the
difference between the two organizations.

LC

Right, they had tracked the split, maybe?

MF

Yeah. And that says a lot. Whereas right-wing sources like
Breitbart, they don't have any idea. They were constantly confusing
the two of us and they probably still do. We also really made an
effort in reaching out to the other Freedom Road and showing our
solidarity, like, we're not in the same organization, but the left
needs to come together and support folks that are being targeted
by the FBI. There could have been really serious consequences for
that. Thankfully, none of them did prison time. But I'm sure it was
hugely stressful and difficult. I mean, I think there are still some
people who feel pretty bitter about the name issue, the fact that they
[the other Freedom Road] just never changed it. But I can imagine
that from their perspective, they're like, "Why should we be the
ones to? Why don't you do it?" You know? And eventually we did.

LC

Actually, I keep thinking about something you said earlier about
the old guilt and shame aspect from the previous group, Fire By

Night. I've been thinking a lot about that in terms of how people react to criticism personally, but in groups too. I think people feel ashamed when they have a misstep, but organizations seem to feel this kind of shame and collective repression. We just don't talk about that problem. We don't want to have to think about these sorts of things you're kind of talking about, like external-internal things. I don't know if you thought about that, the way that guilt or shame play into our responses on an organizational level.

MF

Yeah, I think it's very interesting. I'm thinking back to a conversation when I was on the National Executive Committee (NEC) five or six years ago at one of our meetings, where we were talking about criticism and self-criticism and the practice and process, and it sort of intersecting with some of our members' experience doing generative somatics work.

LC

That's like body response work?

MF

Yeah, there's the body piece, but then also having an awareness of our conditioning, how we've been conditioned or habituated to respond, and what shape we assume, as individuals and as an organization, what shape we show up with. Generative somatics was developed by movement people. It was about bringing somatics into understanding social movement organizations. So at my job at the Chinese Progressive Association (CPA), we've worked with generative somatics. In terms of criticism/self-criticism, the process doesn't necessarily account for people's conditioned responses. So it's like someone showing up who has different condition tendencies, such as the appeasing tendency. There are the people who kind of lean in, like, "Oh, let me help make this better." Then there are those who take a fighting stance. They say that for most people, one of those responses are dominant. But then also, I know for myself that I grew up in a very conflict-averse family—you don't put things on the table. You don't engage in conflict. And if you do, it's very uncomfortable. You just repressed it. It is like stoicism. And so I just remember one of my comrades talking about his life, his experience with generative somatics, and his reflections around the limitations of criticism/self-criticism. But when you don't take those things into account—the shame and the guilt—the conditioning around, like, "Oh, something's uncomfortable, we're going to turn away from it." I think that exists in an organization as well, rather than like, "Let's face this, let's actually bring some light to it, make it more transparent." And in some ways, it could lose some of its power or hold if we do that, rather than pretending, as you said, something doesn't exist, it didn't happen. I was trying to think of certain examples of that as well, of ways that manifests…

LC

Yeah, I'd be curious. Was that criticism/self-criticism something you all were sort of just getting into as an organization, and then you brought in the generative somatics?

MF

It was never really brought into Liberation Road. Culturally, I would say that there are a lot of our members who would just be like, "What the hell is this?" And so for decades we existed in a culture of practicing criticism and self-criticism. We're comfortable with that. But what is this touchy feely, feel into your body, grounding, centering, you know? Which is interesting because I think a lot of that's generational. A lot of it's just the culture of left organization.

PART II

MF

Sometimes, I'm like, generative somatics can only go so far or allow for so much when there's this sort of perpetual habit of being overstretched and overcommitted and taking on too much.

LC

When your shape is just slumped.

MF

Yeah, at times. So that was interesting. What else to say about criticism? I'll just say that what we were saying about people's lack of either skill or ability, or their hesitancy around offering criticism or feedback to others or to the group as a whole—it seems like that's largely a result of overcompensating for the left, for how things were practiced with criticism and self-criticism. And that's one thing I hope will come out of the LRS summation in the writings; it sounded like it just got really rough. People were kind of torn apart. But I don't know if you've heard these stories.

LC

I mean, I feel like I've heard about the Cultural Revolution version of self-criticism . . .

MF

Right.

LC

Which is like the game of telephone: things are received from the history of communism to my American education. So I don't really have a grasp on how it was actually practiced. And then I sort of become this cliché, you know, and I'm just demeaning people through this practice. I think there was some kind of preconception about that when you were talking about how different people were like, "Wait, isn't that the thing where you kind of all point fingers in a meeting at somebody or something?" It was like, no . . . I actually learned about it through Grace Lee Boggs's piece "Organization Means Commitment," in which she talks about how essential it is for organizations and particularly those formed according to democratic centralism. So what you were talking about earlier was interesting to me in terms of the practice of criticism; self-criticism has its limits. And I think that's kind of what I've been reflecting on in terms of democratic centralism as well. What are the limits within that kind of structural formation around similar issues of being able to raise criticism and suggest changes and transformations within an organization? Was that part of how self-criticism was understood, as part of a larger democratic centralism?

MF

Oh, yeah.

LC

Yeah. So that was kind of the primary organizational ideology?

MF

Yeah, as far as I understand it . . . Just really leaning toward the centralism and not the democratic side of things. And some people, just hearing the stories—and I hope you'll have a chance to talk to some of the older OG folks who were in some of these groups—sometimes there's just a cult of personality, like I said, unquestioning of leaders, and that just creates a really unhealthy dynamic. And if anyone questioned that, it was just crushed. It seems like even though we didn't go through that experience of those really harsh sessions of criticism/self-criticism, we're sort of reaping the consequences of it. These days, shying away from conflict and disagreement. But I think that's beginning to shift. I mean, I see it at my workplace, a real encouragement around feedback and courageous conversations. But I don't know what that looks like in left organizations these days. It's one thing if it's a workplace and people are working together every day. And I'm curious, what it looks like at LeftRoots, for example; they're not doing mass work together, but they probably have a tighter structure. Whereas right now, Liberation Road, we still identify as a cadre organization, but we're not working together on this close basis, every day or every week.

LC

It's so rough on organizing.

MF

I talk to folks from Liberation Road maybe once or twice a month, but we're not working together all that closely at this point.

LC

Yeah. So how does the self-criticism practice exist today?

MF

It doesn't [*laughs*]. In our district, it doesn't. And I don't hear other districts talking about it either. There's certainly some practice around evaluation and understanding where our weaknesses or challenges are. But that's different. So we've kind of lost that practice altogether. Is that because we felt like it wasn't working or it had become too rote? Or is it a liberalism setting in, which it very well could be.

LC

Is there anything that's sort of come in to fill that role? You said evaluations—what's that?

MF

Last year, we had each district or commission develop what we called the "strategic implementation plan." It's taking our national strategy and developing it into a plan for each local area or each commission. So we had that for 2020. And then, at the end of the year, we said, "OK, let's evaluate, let's go through the plan and say, did we actually meet these goals? Do we have the outcomes that we were looking for?" So, yeah, we did do that practice, but again, it feels different. Engaging in some kind of criticism/self-criticism . . . It's interesting to consider picking that up again. Or even just restudying, getting reoriented, and talking about what might look different about the process now.

LC

This is super interesting. I feel like I can kind of get a sense from what you're saying about how people might have started to lose interest in it, even just as a kind of political practice. It seems to be just something people from my generation, and especially younger people, don't know. My formative political experience was Occupy. And that was all about councils and consensus. And there was absolutely no mention of criticism or self-criticism. You know, it wasn't until years later that I learned that this was a big part of so many organizations. So I'm just curious how it completely fell away. And maybe that can be chalked up to what you're saying, the bad vibes that people associated with it.

MF

Yeah, right. That is really interesting. I want to put this on the agenda for the next meeting and talk it over.

LC

What were some of the things I think you were saying earlier about criticism/self-criticism, or maybe it was generative

somatics, that had kind of allowed you to access some real
insights in political work? What were some of those insights,
and what was important to you about them?

MF

Yeah, I think probably the process around generative somatics
and just really being able to look at myself through that lens, of
the condition or tendency I have to appease. I'm always trying to
fix things or lean into it, like, "Oh, let me take care of that." And
just understanding how that's not helpful for the organization.
Just being able to understand through that lens.

One aspect of generative somatics is assessment, having
a container for sharing observations with others or being able
to hear an assessment from others—to receive it in a way that
helps to think about how it is that I'm showing up in the work
and how it's translating, what the impact is on the broader
goal, too. Then I think, I'm in my late forties, I've been doing
movement work for a good while now. I imagine that I'm going
to do it for the rest of my life. I think there is an understanding
that we have different relationships to it at different points in our
lives and, you know, overwork, this sort of voluntaristic way of
thinking, like, "Oh, if I just do more." But that actually doesn't
result in any qualitative difference in moving the bar, in moving
the revolutionary process ahead in any kind of way.

It's really clear that without organization it's kind of a given
that most of us will individually move to the right as we get older,
especially those like me, like someone in a place of privilege, who
could easily drift away without being rooted in an organization.
And so, it doesn't mean that I have to be giving myself 150 percent
all the time. No one's asking that of me, and I don't need to put that
on myself. I do plan to stay with this for the rest of my life, you
know? So for the long haul, it's just understanding that arc, but the
long arc of it. Whereas I think when I was younger, because of my
tendency around appeasing, I felt like I had to do everything, I was
just like, "I'm not revolutionary enough" because I'm not showing
up for this, that, or the other. Whereas none of that thinking exists
for me anymore.

LC

That sounds very freeing.

MF

Yeah, it is. And you know, I work in finance. It was not a chosen area of work . . . [*laughs*] I thought, you could do this for the rest of your life; you always have a job, now that you have this skill and experience. And yet, for me, I think there is a period of time when I was like, "I don't want to do this. This is not interesting work." And I sort of came back around to it. My coworker was just talking about this, the infrastructure and the operations work—it's not separate from political work. It's actually very integral. And whereas I think some of the younger people who come into it might think of it as separate from the organizing work, it isn't. I understand that this is something I bring—and it's a very important thing to bring in—that I actually want to help cultivate or support the development of for other people. And as a white person, I think this is an appropriate role for me. I mean, it's interesting because I sort of have moments of like, "Should I be doing organizing work with white communities to undermine white supremacy?" I'm not doing that. It's like, I've chosen a different path and I feel pretty good, I feel confident about that choice. That was definitely wandering away from your original question, but that's what we're doing.

LC

It made me think of all the infrastructural work. It made me think about this argument I've seen come up in groups where people get frustrated by us doing a lot of internal work, or a lot of accounting for group dynamics, and it's like, "Oh, this is taking away from the real work or from the political work." Does that concern ever come up with criticism/self-criticism? Because the whole idea is that you're having this conversation to reflect on the practice in order to transform it. But does that seem like a valid critique to you, that we kind of get stuck on the process and not enough on the enactment?

MF

The navel-gazing. I think there's probably a line to place to balance that. You could go overboard and just be so incredibly focused on that process and that sort of internal reflection. And just thinking of praxis or the process of like . . . for the sake of what? Why are we engaging in criticism/self-criticism? It's to show up in this work as better revolutionaries. To be able to shift the possibility of actually being able to move forward. And without addressing conflicts or internal contradictions, there are real consequences . . . I mean, we know that those contradictions have led to certain organizations folding completely. Or staying stagnant and losing relevance. And that's not doing any service to anyone.

So if you don't face what you know, what's the alternative? The only way you can move through those contradictions is through some kind of process that allows you to face it, to process it, and to rectify and determine a way forward. But I think an acknowledgment of what it is that people show up with—whether it's trauma, and there may be triggering things about the process—that's maybe what needs to shift.

And back to that original thing of the generative somatics . . . it's really about understanding those triggers and what it is that people are showing up with. So what kind of process or container do you have for people to be able to share that, to help inform? I don't know what that would look like but I think that's important.

LC

Something about criticism/self-criticism seems obviously very focused on contradiction and internal contradiction. Maybe that focus can kind of limit the conversation? Does that seem accurate?

MF

This focus on the internal contradictions?

LC

The focus on that as the site of study. For me, thinking about criticism/self-criticism, it's like trying to identify internal contradictions, but also, at the same time, you might just be annoyed by something, you know? [*laughs*] So how do you resolve what's actually up for discussion and criticism?

MF

Right. Right. And sort of unpacking the layers of why that thing annoys you; there's something in your history or whatever, your shape. Some people may not be annoyed by it at all, but you're really annoyed by it. It's like in relationships, there's stuff like that, like, "Oh, that's why that bothers you so much." I think part of what's difficult if you don't have a kind of foundation of trust or . . . And I think in left organizations that doesn't always exist, there isn't necessarily a relationship; it's like, you're sort of in this organization together and if you're not working together, how do you build that relationship? And then the possibility of people being able to talk about what it is they're bringing to the table—that influences the process.

PART III

LC

You were saying you're seeing a shift in the workplace, and that seems to be because you have to see these people every day and there's an urgency or easily identifiable common cause, and that has been evacuated from the left. This could be one reason a practice or program developed from prior leftist orgs such as criticism/self-criticism has fallen out of use. We also see that this practice is taken up in different ways. The buzzword we're doing this project around is "accountability." That seems to be what organizations think about—both nonprofits and leftist organizations have accountability processes rather than something described as a practice of criticism/self-criticism. But it's just interesting, the fact that coworkers almost create more of a bond of necessity for that than the bond we have in leftist organizations. Why don't we have those things in these organizations anymore? What happened?

MF

What does it mean to be a comrade? Something has been lost, and it's not to say it can't be regained, but . . .

LC

It's a category that people want to resurrect, but the material basis or the spiritual basis for it seems to just not really be there for people to truly identify as comrades.

MF

Yeah, that's true.

LC

Do you think there is a moment in which you can locate that loss, or has it been kind of gradual in your experience, such that we didn't necessarily notice a rupture?

MF

It feels more gradual, really. At Liberation Road, people drift off or people leave the organization, and sometimes, many times, some of us don't even know it and, at the same time, others join. I've been in this group with them for twenty years and now they've left. But also, we have national meetings and people will be on Zoom, so just because someone isn't there doesn't mean they've left. And yet, eventually, it's just like, "Well, what happened to this person?" These are people I did feel a comradely connection with, after being in a group with them for twenty years.

LC

That's such a long time.

MF

Yeah, so it's like, is there any process with the leadership, of summation or evaluation that happens jointly between the leadership and that person who left? Something like an exit interview? Because it's a big deal when you lose people. I wouldn't say there are a ton of people who have left, but there are some, and I think there's some that are probably still in and still connected to local work. As I said, people over many years have a different relationship to the organization as it grows. If you're going to be in a group for forty years, it'll look different at different times in your life. But yeah, comrade—what does that mean and how do we create that? How do we cultivate that material and spiritual connection?

LC

Do you all call each other comrade, still?

MF

Yeah, we do.

I feel like even at Pinko, the collective doesn't necessarily call each other comrade, but we kind of have the sense of Pinko as being a project between dispersed comrades.

MF

Are people all over the country or mainly in New York?

LC

Now, it's mostly in New York. But the contributors and people we collaborate with, anybody who's interested in Pinko, we're like, "Become a part, do something with us," because it's that search for communist comrades, at the end of the day. And maybe it'll become the kind of organizational form. You know, you're saying that being in an organization is almost a form of being accountable to a larger political movement or to the revolution. That sounds so right to me in terms of what's often missing in this talk of accountability. It's often individuals being accountable to each other. But what's interesting about something like criticism/self-criticism, what I was teasing out in that parallel was that it seems to be about taking individual accountability to this larger level. And there's also been this problem I've seen where I'm accountable to my comrades in my community, but then when somebody raises a criticism, they're no longer your comrades. You don't have to be accountable to them. So it's kind of a self-serving apology. I don't know what the word would be for it. But yeah, I would be accountable to you, but you're criticizing me, so I don't have to be.

MF

Right, that's true.

LC

It feels sad when organizations fracture, even though I know they often need to, or that it's gotten to a point where things break. It seems like you try to to be accountable to the organization, but at a certain point it almost feels like it has to break.

MF

Right, yeah, and I've had moments in Liberation Road when it's like, if something doesn't change or there isn't a real shift, then

I'm not sure this is the place to put my energy, and yet I'm still here. To me it comes back to the question of organization and the importance of being in an organization. It's not to say that we've dealt with all those challenges or contradictions, they still very much exist.

LC

It's just fascinating to hear about how organizations have structured themselves. One thing I thought was important about Freedom Road/Liberation Road was the integration of anarchists, anarchists who were seemingly curious about nihilism or even kind of transitioning into Maoism. Do you think that kind of shifted the process around criticism/self-criticism, or was it sort of like, "No, we're into that and we don't need to change it?" Is there a kind of anarchist tradition that's similar or any kind of similar process? Were you involved? Because you were more involved in anarchist organizing before, no?

MF

Not really. I mean, Fire By Night came out of anarchism, but we never really identified as anarchists. I probably did individually at some point, but I wasn't tied to any organization. Ward Churchill was one of my professors at Boulder, so I think I was really influenced by his anti-Marxism for a long period. It's part of my political formation. So, I kind of moved towards anarchism partly for that reason.

You know, that's a good question, if there is a similar tradition within anarchism. I don't actually know. I wonder. I wouldn't be surprised if they actually practiced some form of criticism/self-criticism in Love and Rage. I'd be interested.

LC

And now, like you're saying, organizing has been so strange during the pandemic. Something about the isolation, I think, has created more fodder for conflict or misunderstanding.

MF

Yeah, that's true.

LC

Have you seen any of those kinds of effects? Not necessarily
in your organization, but . . . there were just a lot of scene
implosions in New York, and a lot of it had to do with, I'm not
sure exactly, but I think in part from the conditions of isolation
for many during lockdown.

MF

I'm trying to think if I've seen it. I'm not surprised to hear that,
like you said, fodder . . . But I'm trying to think if I have seen
that happen. I haven't heard about much.

LC

I guess we'll just be fighting differently again [*laughs*].

MF

The organization where I work, we're doing really well with
it, but we're onboarding people like during shelter-in-place,
everybody's working remotely. It's really tough conditions for
building a foundation of trust.

LC

Yeah, that trust aspect . . . I think that must be a part of the
reason people find it so hard to criticize others, they don't
think that there's something . . . they don't trust the other
person won't take it personally. My partner has always said
that's a very American thing. And yeah, maybe. I've only
ever organized in the States, so . . . there does seem to be
something. Maybe white American culture in particular. Don't
shake the boat kind of mentality. Did you all ever use the word
"accountability" or is that not really part of the movement
vocabulary for Liberation Road?

MF

Yes. It's a good question. I'm sure it was used at some point,
but it was not common parlance. I think we want to ensure that
comrades are doing what they say they're going to do. I mean,
we probably used it to some degree. The importance of people
staying accountable to what, you know? What's been agreed
to, and following through. I think that probably the strategic
implementation plan . . . there was a degree of like, OK, because

we had to sort of list out who's going to be doing what, how do we remain accountable to each other around the plan? I mean, it's just interesting to see here again at CPA; I think we're really committed to accountability, but also there's a lot of discussion about the importance of making mistakes, because only through mistakes do we learn. That's one way that we grow. So actually, I feel like there's this culture of encouragement around mistakes, making mistakes, taking risks, and getting things wrong. It's a learning curve, and there's no shame. So that's been really interesting and important, I think, as a supervisor. One of the people I supervise started last summer and she came in kind of terrified of making mistakes. And I really instituted this, that we are going to make mistakes. I make them all the time. And most of the time it's all correctable. Yes, there may be an impact. And we acknowledge that and we rectify the issue. But it's OK. And maybe someone will respond in a harsh way or a way that doesn't feel good. But it's all just part of a process of learning.

LC

That seems like a good way to go about things. I've never experienced that outside of CPA . . .

MF

Yeah, right.

LC

This attitude that you foster seems so healthy for growth and openness and transparency. Have you experienced that in a political context?

MF

Not as much.

LC

What do you think about that? Why don't we do that?

MF

Again, maybe it's the work culture versus a political organization, even though it looks a little bit different if we're doing collective work together, right? Why not?

LC

I mean, maybe the stakes feel different. You know, it's a little bit harder for a leftist group to say, "We made a mistake," if they're already coming from a compromised position overall. Maybe that's one reason for the kind of declining interest in or practice of criticism/self-criticism, that things are just too hard to face right now because of the state of organization.

MF

Yeah, and if you were to frame a criticism/self-criticism process in that way, that it's in order to lift up or really bring some awareness to mistakes we've made individually and collectively in order to help us grow, it's not about shaming anyone or berating people.

LC

Or, you know, berating yourself. That seems to be what people actually do these days when it happens. There's something about that guilt and shame that just seems so endemic to the way people are showing up to work and then kind of . . .

MF

Totally. It's not good.

LC

So how do you think you'd bring it up, if you were to, at the next meeting? If you were to raise it, it would kind of be to resurrect the practice, no?

MF

Yeah, I mean, I think I would just say that I've noticed that we've fallen off the practice of criticism/self-criticism for years and that we have engaged in this practice before. It would be really healthy and good for us to pick it back up and to also deconstruct it or reshape it in a way, not so it feels comfortable, but so it feels relevant or rooted in our collective context of this moment. And, you know, we have a range of people; we have someone who has been in for maybe two years, and some of us have been on for a much longer time. So, for the newer person, maybe it's not something they are familiar with or that they have ever done.

LC

But it also sounds like maybe there hasn't been a lot of internal conflict to deal with in a way that criticism/self-criticism can sometimes help with or the accountability process usually swoops in at the moment of. You said that if there hasn't been an alternative way that you think about dealing with conflict, members have some sort of fight or somebody harmed somebody else or something like that.

MF

Yeah, right. Yeah, I mean, our district really hasn't experienced it. Maybe we're just too nice to each other.

LC

California types.

MF

Exactly. Just affirming each other. No criticism. It's like, all understanding all the time. Conflict averse.

LC

Maybe it's not good then that there's been absolutely no conflict. I don't just mean that people work well together, that's a positive obviously, but also no group is above criticism. That being said, at least it hasn't been super harmful to work together.

MF

Yeah, I think a challenge for our district has been that for many years we didn't have collective work we were doing together. So there just wasn't even a basis for conflict, you know? Like, we're not interacting with each other outside of meetings or studies. And that changed somewhat last year, even though last year was 2020—we were doing work together, but it wasn't like we were on phone banks together, like what does that mean? We weren't working really closely on a steering committee or some other organizing body that did intensive work together.

LC

There weren't all those little moments for tension or I want to do it this way but . . .

MF

Yeah, right. Whereas I think in Fire By Night, for example, that looks really different. We were doing intensive work together every weekend. We'd spend all day, pretty much the whole day Saturday and half the day Sunday, together, studying, door-knocking, organizing, developing strategy.

LC

Was that a different energy because of a different sort of political strategy or just the moment and the people?

MF

I mean, all of us of were of a certain age group, no kids, no commitments outside of it. We each had jobs, but they were jobs to pay the rent, put food on the table, not consuming jobs. And so we were in and this was part of building a new left organization, this practice. We were all deeply committed to it.

LC

That's so interesting, it seems then that accountability or personal criticism was not so much about mediating conflicts within the group, but more about moving forward, which sounds more productive.

MF

And to put you hopefully in better practice when there really is something.

Peter Hardie

Peter Hardie is a "65-year-old veteran of a lot
of movements." From his start taking part in a
"vibrant anticolonial movement around the world,"
he joined the Proletarian Unity League, a tendency
coming out of the Students for a Democratic
Society which later became part of the Freedom
Road Socialist Organization (now Liberation Road).
Peter was equally involved in various Black radical
formations. He worked in a factory for a decade
and a half, as staff for the Service Employees
International Union (SEIU), and then in South
Africa as a coordinator for the American Federation
of Labor and Congress of Industrial Organization
(AFL-CIO) affiliate Solidarity Center.

M. E. O'BRIEN

Hello. Why don't you start off, Peter, and introduce yourself
however you like.

PETER HARDIE

Yeah, so my name is Peter Hardie. Sixty-five-year-old veteran of
a lot of movements. Been involved with socialist organizations
from the time I got out of college in '77. And yeah, I've seen a few
things along the way. I'm a father. I'm hoping to retire sometime
soon. And, yeah, trying to sort out what it means to be an elder in
this moment. That's what I will leave it at.

MO

So a lot of the interviews we're doing in Pinko are trying to
think about some of the contradictions and complexities around
ideas of accountability. To start off, what does that word,
accountability, evoke for you?

PH

I guess two phases in my life: On the one hand, when I
became a member of a socialist organization, there was
a certain sense of accountability there that was more
ideological, meaning more in the sense of adherence to
some level of accountability to the people around political
practice, around agreeing to a collective decision-making
process. At some point in the last, I don't know, ten or twenty
years, I think it's changed to mean more of a personal level
trying to think about myself as a cis-heterosexual man. The
privileges entailed in that. And my commitment to grappling
with those, if not overcoming them, to at least acknowledge
that that was a force in my life, and then dealing with that.
And I think that comes from two places. One, when I got to
New York in the 2000s, I was in much more contact with the
queer liberation folks and with nonbinary folks, and realized
how much I didn't know about gender and patriarchy. And
also as someone committed to social change, what it meant
to be accountable to those forces and those movements and
individuals around me. Not just acknowledging everybody
has the right to do their own thing, but also defending and
opposing discrimination and oppression based on patriarchy
or heteropatriarchy.

So I think accountability has definitely changed. I came up in the movement and we were, I don't know, gay-tolerant, maybe, is the right word. I mean, we didn't really understand the gender binary, but we sort of opposed discrimination and oppression on general terms. But I think there's now a sense of needing a greater understanding and struggling for a principled understanding of the lived lives and lived expression and lived politics of people who may or may not be socialists, but are clearly not gender normative or gender normal.

MO

That's interesting, I hear you talk about two meanings of accountability: One, accountability to a group process of democratic centralism and accountability to politics to align a political vision that might be sort of easy to veer off from in the conditions of our lives. And then accountability as an ally in terms of thinking about your privileges and about the emergence of a movement that you might not know tons about. The way that we're approaching it is different than either of those. Mostly, it's thinking about accountability as the internal process of how movements deal with harm. So that might be in Maoist terms—criticism/self-criticism, combat liberalism, unity/struggle/unity—the history of ideas like that. And these days, accountability shows up a lot as a notion in transformative justice, people trying to do alternatives to police and prisons and what that means. But that you brought up these two other meanings, I think, is very interesting, and I'd encourage you to elaborate on them. You said a little bit about trying to think about queerness. Could you say a bit more about the first one? Thinking about accountability to line and to a group and to each other?

PH

So it's interesting you raise this sort of criticism/self-criticism, because I was on a call earlier today talking with younger comrades. Now, there's more attention paid in movement spaces to harm and blind spots, whether it's hetero blindspots or male or patriarchal blindspots. I noted that there's definitely a sense in spaces now that's different from spaces I came up in when I was in my twenties, which were much more sort of criticism/self-criticism as a vehicle for growth and personal change. The reality that I recall—and it may have been just my experience—but the reality was that those spaces, those criticism/self-criticism spaces were very male, cis-hetero dominated. I think to the extent that you had cultures and organizations that were fairly heterosexual, that allowed for the development of cultures that weren't necessarily as open. And on another level, the movement has shifted a little bit, in the sense that democratic centralism and dogmatism are less acceptable. In a good way, meaning the good elements of that. "Let's stick together and work together even if we disagree, and let's find truth where we can find it, whether it's in the writings of Marx or in the writings of Cabral or in the writings of the Combahee River Collective." Let's try to find a theory where we can find it.

So that's all good. But if I think of myself as a cis-hetero man, pronouns are a good example. I know I have to work to remind myself to identify my pronouns. And it's probably not even on this Zoom call, but I changed it for the previous call. Those are the kinds of things that, as a privileged man, I don't think about—the harm I'm doing when I'm mis-gendering people or when I'm not aware that there's all that privilege connected with who I am as a man. So, yeah, I think accountability looked a lot different maybe forty years ago than it does now and people hold each other to standards that are much less about politics and more about how we treat each other as human beings.

MO

That's very interesting. So tell me briefly about your political arc. You mentioned being in a socialist organization since you got out of college in '77. What's the general arc of the major movements you've been a part of?

PH

So I came out of college in the '70s and there was a sort of vibrant anti-colonial movement around the world; corresponding solidarity movements in the United States for struggles happening internationally, like in Angola and the anti-apartheid movement. Personally, I was involved in the politics of decolonizing education in the '70s, so struggling for African American studies, struggling for Chicano studies. I don't know that I was active in the women's studies movement, but I think that it was concurrent with those things as well. When I got out of college, I went into the labor movement and was a factory worker for six or seven years. I got involved in the union where I was and the union's Civil Rights Committee.

But during that same period of time, there was an extensive network of what was called, at the time, the National Black United Front. Boston had a Black United Front; there were Black United Fronts in a number of the major cities. And for the most part they mirrored the Black Panthers, meaning they were trying to target police violence, segregation, and trying to develop a national agenda for Black liberation minded folks around the country. At the same time, I came out of college politicized on the level of class and socialism as well, so I don't know if I can name all the iterations of those organizations, but the Proletarian Unity League was where I found my socialist home. And then, I'd say I split my script, my allegiance to a variety of Black liberation organizations like the Black United Front, the African Liberation Support Committee (ALSC), and the various iterations of those organizations all the time. That may be as much as I can remember.

MO

Sure. And then continuing on, did you stay in the labor movements, the socialist organization, and Black organizing?

PH

Yes and no. I was in labor for about twelve or fourteen years after college, worked in a factory under one union and joined the Service Employees International Union (SEIU), working as a staff-person for public employees in Boston. Most of the national formation stuff and the Black liberation movement I was connected to ebbed and flowed like everything else. There was the National Black United Front. It was ALSC at a certain point. There was the Black Radical Congress. So we were traveling to Mississippi to work with anti-racist, active organizing in Mississippi. So yeah, I've stayed involved to this day. I still consider myself a socialist and I still consider myself a revolutionist and a Black liberationist as well. And those things have evolved.

You know, I think I would say I'm probably clearer about patriarchy now than I was for quite a number of those years. And it goes back—we knew that some of the Black liberation movements of the '60s were very patriarchal and some homophobic, although not as much as people tend to think. But I think it's been a little bit of a journey for me as an older activist in my forties and fifties to start to think about the interconnection between patriarchy or heteropatriarchy, capital, and white supremacy. So my political growth has probably brought me to a sharper understanding of the relationship and the importance of centering all three and not just the class or the race struggle.

But, yeah, I've stayed involved. I'm working with Black Lives Matter activists in Louisville, Kentucky, a little bit here in D.C. I was overseas for a while, so my activism was muted in the sense that I was doing some work in South Africa related to labor there and just sort of mindful of the political growth of South Africa as a former apartheid state and colony and trying to understand the international economy and the impact on states like South Africa.

MO

So Pinko is interested in both formal and informal practices of dealing with internal harm and conflict and abuse in movements, and it would probably make sense to talk about the movements a little bit separately. It sounds like they have a little bit of separation in your life, even if they're in dialogue with each other. I mean, I know you most from your work in the legacy of the New Communist Movement. Do you have a sense of what you would like to talk about or what would be interesting to talk about, to start off, around both informal and formal ways of dealing with internal conflict and harm?

PH

So a couple of things come up. One is, we make a lot of assumptions in this work, and so if you leave aside the sort of New Communist Movement, even the sort of Black civil rights struggle, the Black Power movement—you have organizations like the Black Panthers that articulated, whether they were practicing or not, a certain understanding of the need for allyship and political alliance around the struggle against capital and empire. You had a little bit less of that, actually, in the civil rights movement. I'm not the best person to give an analysis of that, but I think what that results internally is a whole lot of tension that doesn't get affirmed or actualized around male practices, around heterosexual practices in relationship to people. And so, while the Panthers may have espoused a certain level of early alliance with gay liberation forces back then, there certainly wasn't a lot of evidence of homosexual or queer Black folks engaged fully in the Black Panthers. So a lot of that harm gets hidden, you know; we don't know what it was because we don't know and nobody was interested in it. That's changed a good bit recently, and I'm trying to think about the interim period, but the rise of Black Lives Matter, for example, was the result of three queer women, and we're still grappling with that—meaning, I think a lot of men in movement spaces are working on it and in a lot of good ways, on our understanding of it, while in a lot of other spaces, they're not.

There's still a certain level of if not outright homophobia or misogyny, frankly, then a certain sense that people are not interested in talking about it. And so, as a result, you've had powerful voices of women and queer and trans women shaping the dialogue, forcing the movement to grapple with them as human beings and to grapple with the kinds of oppressions they faced as part and parcel, or at least connected to the struggle against white supremacy. Sometimes I chafe at that a little bit because, in some ways, in a lot of ways, I'm old-school in terms of studying. But I think there is some new knowledge coming up that's not based in the literature of the revolutions or the literature of the New Communist Movement, but that is based in the real-life experiences of people who decided that they are tired of oppression and, whether they have the same understanding that I do or not, want to do something about it. So, yeah, I would say those spaces have changed, the Black liberation spaces have changed for the good, but they're not there yet and we still have a lot of work to do now.

MO

In the queer spaces that I'm in, the queer and trans political spaces I mean, there are extremely sophisticated discussions about transformative justice and addressing harm and lots of other things. And frankly, I think they might have something to learn from criticism/self-criticism, combat liberalism, unity/struggle/unity—there are some old-school principles that, one,

I think might have had more influence on the present moment than people realize and, two, might have moments in them of clarity and helpfulness that people could use. So part of what we wanted to do in these interviews is think about the two together, think about different currents of accountability and not just be, "Oh, this one's new and cool and made by queers and the other stuff is old school and boring and made by men." But to actually have a little bit more of a dialogue between them, more thinking about them alongside each other, or thinking about how they might have influenced each other in ways that people don't always talk about. So that's part of what I mean—I appreciate all the self-critical, self-reflective things you're saying about gender and patriarchy and sexuality. But I would also encourage you to actually share what worked and what didn't work and what you all were trying to do in these spaces, in Black liberation spaces, communist movement spaces.

PH

That's a very good point. And I agree with you 100 percent. On some level there was a certain value system connected with criticism/self-criticism that maybe, though not always, engendered a certain amount of trust that these were the kinds of things you could talk about in self-criticism, and these were not. Parallel to that, I think there's just been a certain weakness in ideology and in ideological perspective around what we're trying to do. The immediate example that comes to mind is that it's a simple thing to organize and rant against oppression as a thing that's affecting me. Trans women, the murder of trans women, for example, has been in the news and there's a lot of discussion about that. But it's not really connected, in analysis, to some of the bigger things that we think are important. And so that's not unusual, I mean, the struggle around white supremacy in the Black community is often more about white bias and white prejudice and discrimination. And I can't get a house in this neighborhood or, you know, I want to start a business, and not connected to real political analysis of where oppression comes from and how trans-oppression or queer oppression or patriarchy or white supremacy are connected to the capitalists, the global capitalist, neoliberal capitalism.

I feel like that's a weakness I do see in a lot of movement spaces . . . What's good is that there's a lot of attention on how we behave with each other. And I think that's important and good, and to the extent that some of this is about building community that can move together, then you need to build community. You can't just move together. It doesn't just happen. On the other hand, where are we moving, what are we moving? I think that's the weakness there has been in political study. And I grapple with that because there's a certain amount of privilege connected to political study that is allowed to students and intellectuals of various sorts, and that doesn't always get pushed down into the streets.

On the other hand, if we're not clear about what we're fighting and we're not clear about the connections between the various struggles, then we're sort of floating around in this area of, "I don't want to be harmed," and we're calling people out for harming and we don't always—and this is my experience particularly in some Black movement spaces— we're not always clear about how we're trying to build and move the struggle. I think you're right, I mean, I'm not sure I have a coherent thought around this, but I do feel, to a great extent, an anticapitalist element is not being woven in where it needs to be woven in. I would say that that should be the legacy of the socialist movement: We should have done a better job. But I think some of it is also just that every generation creates its own terrain and struggle. We have an obligation to try to figure out how to help. I mean, the question of accountability is always a question of accountability for what? Are we all in the same struggle? By that, I mean that we are fundamentally, but some of us are less interested in the struggle against patriarchy, or only see the struggle against white supremacy, and don't see capitalism as a key target for liberation. And socialists ultimately have to hold each other and the movement's feet to the fire on all three. Accountability for upholding all three facets/fronts of struggle.

MO

Yeah, that really makes a lot of sense in that there's such intense arguments right now between, "Oh, this is bad cancel culture," or, "Oh, you're enabling abuse," that is all focused on behavior and not, "What are the political stakes of what we're fighting for and how does this help us get there or hinder us from getting there?" And that's to sort of draw back to your first point about accountability to politics, to a political vision on some level, or to a critique of capitalism. Would you be up for talking a little bit about criticism/self-criticism and how it worked; what you saw and what worked and what didn't?

PH

Yeah. I think I did notice that, at least in the early days, women were more subject to criticism than men. And not really about the level of productivity or hours put in. More just about stuff, lack of understanding. I think some of that was student days, and so, you know, nobody's really doing anything or raising families or working a real job. And then once folks were in a factory or we were doing community organizing, I think the criticism did shift to more systemic stuff, i.e., not a criticism of you as an individual for X, Y, or Z, but more, "How do we critique ourselves? How do we try to understand lessons from our work? What works, what doesn't work? What should we do tomorrow that we didn't do today or what shouldn't we do tomorrow that we did do today?" And so, I think it's a tool for growth and maybe accountability, in the sense of being true to the work and being honest about the work. Not just doing stuff because everybody else is doing it, but really trying to figure out if we're actually serving the people or just serving ourselves. That's the sort of blanket statement, and I think it may or may not be true in all instances.

I don't recall the last time a person was called on the carpet. I think we have been gentler with each other over the past few decades. And I think that is a result of, one, the struggle of people who aren't male and white against the behaviors of people who are male and white, and two, the communist movement, I think, has been committed to trying to grapple with some of that stuff, even if it's only words. But I think it's sunk in, in some places. Right now I'm in a study group with some men in the Louisville, Kentucky, area to try to grapple with masculinity and what it means to be male in female-led, and women-led, queer women–led movements. Just trying to think through that, I mean, trying to figure out how to be disciplined, how to appreciate and acknowledge and follow the leadership of non-male non-men. And the counter-education that we have to do as men against all the sort of not only legit—when I say legit, actual political forces out there of male supremacy in our community, in the Black community—but also against the invisible cultural pushes of men to be in control, to see only weakness in women, to "other" queer and trans men and women. It's been an interesting experience. I mean, I think people are trying to do it and we're sort of struggling through it.

But yeah, I do feel like there is value in criticism/self-criticism, to the extent that in the same way we think about oppression as systemic and not just about individual people, we've got to think about critique and self-critique as not just, Peter Hardie, what did you do right today and what did you do wrong today, but self-critique of ourselves as a revolutionary force, an actual force for actual change. What is required of us as a community/collective—was what *we* did the right thing to do? The wrong thing to do? How do we think about what we do tomorrow? More time on strategy, and less time on negotiating theory or ideology. A lot of movement spaces tend to get dominated by stuff that clearly tells you that people are really fighting the same thing and that, wow, maybe all those struggles are important and need to be dealt with. That we can't keep people on the basis of just resolving your particular grievance with somebody else; that if we're trying to build a movement, we've got to have some values that allow us to raise criticisms and expect that they'll be dealt with, rather than raise criticisms as a way to point out all the problems of the world. I mean, I grapple with this a lot around the white socialist movement in relation to the Black liberation movement. And this constant sort of railing about white leftists and white anarchists in the white white white . . . and that, one, they're not all white, and two, they're not all . . . you know, the anarchists are not all white either. But it's easy to sort of create the straw man, the straw person, and rail against the influence of so-called whites on movement spaces that are dominated by people of color, African Americans.

And my attitude is, if we're clear about who we're fighting, then we're clear about the need for allies, and if we're clear about the need for allies, then we're clear about the need for discussion with those allies. It's not just like we make demands of allies; we're in a movement together and we have to sort of negotiate, navigate some collective space and roles and viewpoints and accept some things that we may or may not 100 percent agree with them on.

MO

Can you remember a specific example of criticism/self-criticism that stands out to you or that had an impact on you?

PH

The one that stands out was really a sort of attack on a particular woman. I don't remember all the details, but it just sort of felt like ganging up. And again, this was sort of in the "criticism is personal" as opposed to "criticism as organizational" period. It was mean-spirited and it was really sort of . . . I'd love to be able to say I wasn't a part of it, I don't even remember whether I was or was not. I just remember talking to the woman afterward and feeling like she was right; she felt hurt and betrayed and probably left the movement. Or at least left the organization. And I think that had a big impact on me in terms of, one, thinking about the relationship between theory and people's lived experience, the understanding that theory was not enough to really make what happened happen. That her lived experience and her perspective was not even ignored, but just sort of suppressed and denied and that's not . . . that's a place of privilege to do that, to deny someone's perspective, that's a place of privilege and that I'm a very privileged man. I went to college and worked plenty of jobs. And, you know, I haven't experienced the levels of insecurity or hatred or discrimination or violence that many people have. Criticism should be a shared vehicle as opposed to a weapon. So that's what I remember. My memory is terrible actually. You've got more out of my memory than probably most people have.

MO

Any examples of it being used as a vehicle? Maybe from the later period, of people beginning to try to think about criticism in an organizational- or movement-wide way?

PH

I think there are quite a few . . . The organization has grappled with a lot of changes in policy and practice. Should people go south and work in the South, the development of chapters in places like San Diego and where our forces have been able to grow and where they haven't been able to grow, and what is that a result of. There's been good conversations about what we've been able to do, and I feel like even the sort of criticism that's come up about where we are, or are not connected to Occupy, are we or are we not connected to Black Lives Matter. And should we be leading those things. Those are good conversations to have and they don't have clean answers. Putting all this together is going to be a matter of getting beyond organizational boundaries and really thinking about the big, broad, united front stuff that we've talked about and promoted as part of our political line. And then, it's testing it on a daily basis and trying to figure that out. We're better at that now than we were.

I think we're still figuring some other things out too. You know, how to move political education and spaces that are not our own. A good example was, this afternoon we had a study session with a bunch of young potential members. They had questions about any number of our stuff, and I think we tried to balance, on the one hand, how and why we got here with some sense that the perspectives of people who are critical or unsure, that those perspectives are real, too, and that we're unsure. A lot of us are unsure. We shape this theory and we shape our practice on a day-to-day basis. So what we wrote ten years ago, we're happy to repudiate. I think that's what legitimate criticism/ self-criticism is, which is to say, we're learning and we need to think about learning. There's a dearth of learning in a lot of organizations. On the one hand, people are bemoaning the fact that we lose a strike or we lose an organizing campaign and we don't even make time to learn what happened? So I sort of feel that's important to me, that's the sort of kernel of criticism/self-criticism, which is, can we learn, what can we learn, and are we making that a regular practice?

MO

Are there other ways of dealing with internal harm in movements that you've witnessed or that have had an impact on you, formal or informal?

PH

Yeah. I think I've learned the most by actually listening to the voices of victims or survivors of patriarchy and heteropatriarchy. As you go back, you find the critiques of the civil rights movement, you find the critiques of the Black Panther movement. BLM right now is engaged in a serious internal reckoning. The movement is growing and I think most of that is the strengthening of the voices that have not been heard. Queer, trans women's voices that have just not been heard. And that's where we sort of gain some strength, both in practical organizing, but also in understanding what we're grappling with.

The last few years, I've been leaning more into patriarchy as the main danger, rather than capitalism as the main danger. And I don't have enough of a theoretical understanding to answer that question, but just because you start seeing the ravages of patriarchy, both globally as well as here in the United States, you can't help but wonder whether we're ever going to have a better world if we can't solve patriarchy. It flies under the radar of a lot of leftists because they think it's sort of related, or the domain of some other sort of groupings of women or queers or trans or whatever. Fifty percent of the world is non-male and non-white, probably more actually, non-male and non-white anyway, and they're developing their own sense of what's going on in the world, independent of socialist theory or anybody else's theory. We need to be in movement with those forces that maybe don't come out of our theoretical head of heritage. And yeah, it's going to be work. It will be fruitful. The answers lie there, they don't lie in our heads, and they definitely don't lie in the heads of men. They don't. They definitely don't lie there.

MO

This conversation is very theoretically and politically interesting. It feels a little abstract. A lot of what you've been talking about is your own learning and the collective learning of a lot of men around thinking about gender and sexuality. Can you think of something concrete from your experience, like where you've hurt somebody or seen a man hurt somebody and watched people deal with that, that you learned from at the time?

PH

What first comes to mind is dysphoria. I'm still not sure I understand it. That's the wrong way to say, but I've struggled with that, because I've sort of felt, OK, if gender is a construct, then does it matter what your body looks like? But I've been around enough trans folks to start challenging my own thinking about that. So even if I don't understand it, I try to, and I also acknowledge that it doesn't matter whether I understand it or not. It's an acknowledged experience of people that I know, and yeah, that's fine and good and so that's the first thing that came to my mind. I probably live in a little bit more of a bubble than most, and there hasn't been a lot of sort of active movement space in the last five or ten years that hasn't been dominated by women and or femmes.

MO

I mean, I've seen four organizations torn apart in the last three years because of sexual assault. Destroyed. Just destroyed. They're gone. There were accusations, probably well-founded, around sexual assault. There was a discovery of a cover-up or whatnot. And the biggest anti-police brutality coalition of ultra leftists in New York was torn apart this summer. You know, one of the main ultra left magazines was closed around it. One of the biggest student-based socialist organizations in the United States was gone. The biggest British socialist organization, totally gone. I feel like this stuff is just happening right and left and people don't know what to do. I mean, the shutting down of an organization is sometimes what needs to happen. And those harms of sexual assault are things that have happened in every movement. People are trying to figure out how to deal with them. And it's a hell of a lot better than not dealing with them. There's something very unique and special about sexual assault, but it's also on a continuum of a lot of other things that happen in movements that people are trying to grapple with.

PH

Yeah. I mean, I know of many of those instances. I've read about them. I haven't been in close proximity with them. And it may be that some of those things happened in my organization and it's been hushed up, I don't know for a fact.

MO

Well, if it hasn't come up in your group, do you think there is a reason that you all have managed to avoid it? Is there a different culture around working with gender or working with interpersonal harm, where maybe it hasn't happened as much as it might have happened elsewhere?

PH

It's a good question. I don't know. If I were to take a stab at
it, I think most of the people who are sort of my age or who
came in around the same time I did, everybody sort of coupled
up. Probably not entirely true. I mean, I do remember some
relationships that split up. I think we took the study of male
supremacy fairly seriously. It was one of the first studies I
remember in college. You know, it was sort of a combination
of both. It wasn't quite as sophisticated as more recent stuff
around patriarchy or heteropatriarchy, but it was pretty clear
that socialists didn't behave in certain ways. Lefties are some
of the most abusive and intolerable people in a lot of spaces
here and elsewhere around the globe. Which, I don't know . . .
I don't assume that we're necessarily better, I just assume that
we've been luckier. I'd have to think about that, I don't want to
presume that somehow we've answered some questions that
other people have struggled with. On the other hand, you're
right. I mean, I don't think we've had that level of stuff . . .

MO

I remember when I helped write the gender unity document.
And there was a line in there that states if it's suspected that there's
a pretty reasonable likelihood that someone might have committed
sexual assault, they'd be thrown out of the organization. I was
worried that that would be super controversial. And there were
other things that were controversial in the document. But on
that point, everyone says, "We've thrown people out for less. Sure.
Yeah, of course, we'd throw them out." And I say, "Oh, OK.
Well, that's cool."

PH

Yeah, I mean, I think you're right, there is a little bit of a . . .
We've managed to attract a broad spectrum of people to the
organization, and I think some of that is just sort of the character
and style and culture of our organization. I think we are open
to criticism. I mean, I feel like we don't resist criticism. And it
may not be that we understand or accept or follow through on
it it all the time, but I think people can raise criticisms and they
get accepted as not counterrevolutionary, but they get accepted
as, "OK, let's think about that" at least, or, "Let's deal with it"
at best. And I do feel like that's the culture of our organization.

Some of that is a culture of respect, meaning . . . maybe we're a little less hierarchical. I don't know, that's a good question. You're raising some good questions. I think there may be a level at which we're not as hierarchical as a lot of the other sort of socialist left organizations where, you know, they've got a chairman of a central committee. There may be something to that. And that may be related a little bit more to trying to be democratic, and at the same time, I think we've moved away from centralism toward more democracy. That's reflected in our Congresses and in our chapters here in the area. That's a good point. Actually, I hadn't thought about that.

MO

I remember one serious conflict in one branch and the national, and pointing a couple of people to look into it, to sort of talk to everyone involved, and try to get an assessment of what was happening and try to figure out if it could be resolved and what that would take and if there was any serious, serious, destructive behavior on anyone's part. That's a formal process of dealing with harm and conflict. I feel like there are these threads, these ways of trying to deal with it, trying to address it that could lead to a sort of cover-up or something like that, but could also lead to something very positive. Most of the time, in the history of the organization that I saw, which is a very small window of time, just—what was it—five years or six years that I was there with you all, that people made a sincere effort to deal with conflicts that came up.

PH

This gets back to the question of who are the enemies of the people and who are friends of the people, and being clear about being able to distinguish that, just because someone might be completely fucked up it doesn't necessarily make them an enemy of the people, and balancing that with how much harm they are doing or can do or actually do? To protect other folks, I mean. Racists can be harmful, and people with racist views can be harmful, but they are not all enemies of the people. How do we manage differences, how do we grow a new society? We have to think beyond that. I mean, I think you're saying the same thing I'm thinking, which is: I think we have had an approach more along the lines of, "How do you reconcile differences

among the people? How do we call people into something,
as opposed to just call them out and kick them out, or split?"
That doesn't serve anybody, and frankly, it's been the tool of
government and covert agencies to disrupt movement-building.
That said, a lot of harm has been done inside movements, and
it's a good thing that it's recognized, it's a good thing that people
ensure the safety of all. Building and safeguarding community.

MO

And sometimes protecting and caring for people means making
sure that folks do leave.

PH

Exactly, exactly. I think the Native Americans had a practice—
they didn't have capital punishment—but for very, very, very
serious crimes, they send people off into the wilderness and
say, you know, you can come back in two years, but you can't
be around here. And I think that's legitimate. To the extent
that we've got to interrogate our own systems to make sure
that they're not replicating some of the same harm in how
we evaluate harm. But that's important to do as well, and in
some ways why we need to have the folks—at the intersection
of most stuff in the leadership of things and in the center of
thinking about what harm is and what it means and how we
should deal with it—the people who've been harmed repeatedly
and the most. Yeah, I mean, some of this is we're trying to
shovel sand off the beach in the face of the ocean. Some of us
have the privilege of even thinking about it, and a lot of people,
not us maybe, but a lot of people don't have that privilege and
don't even have time to think about some of these things. And
so we've got to get good at helping folks, say, when they're
harmed and saying . . .

One of the things we were talking about today was just how
do you start meetings. And I said that you used to start meetings
by asking, how's everybody doing and who needs some help
with anything? Every meeting, anywhere, everywhere with
whoever—who needs help and what help can we give you and
how can we help you? So that people understand that it's OK
to ask for help and it's OK to say something's wrong. Because
privileged people don't have as many things that are wrong or
are harming them, and so it's easier to start a meeting with "Let's

get down to business la-da-da." Meanwhile, people are hurting and they don't want to come back to the meeting because nothing offers them any solace or any help.

And that's—I don't know if it's a lesson for the movement, but it's certainly a lesson for me, which is that movements are not just about issues or ideas, they're really about community and embracing people, embracing each other and learning how to embrace each other, because we don't really know . . . we've been raised not to, we've been raised to be jerks and idiots and mean and hostile. Maybe not all necessarily just those things, but to compete. To defend. To not be vulnerable. We've been raised for all these things, and I think our movements have to change to create something new. Maybe we haven't even imagined it yet.

MO

I've noticed that you have avoided identifying your organization and we are somewhat interested in political lineages and political histories. There are different kinds of socialist organizations in the United States. Could you say a little bit more, in your own words, about your group? If you don't want to identify it, we certainly won't. But to give some sense of kind of where it's coming from?

PH

Yeah, sure. I have no problem with that. So some of it is just that we've changed our name a few times over time. But we're now the Liberation Road Socialist Organization, formerly Freedom Road Socialist Organization (FRSO). Freedom Road comes out of a variety of trends out of the '60s and '70s. Proletarian Unity League is my earliest communist organization, in the late '70s. Folks who have drifted in and out, we have absorbed other organizations, recruited all ages. We're still standing, and many organizations have dissolved. I don't think that's any solace to anybody. But not so sadly, the fact that I think folks who are still committed to a radical change in this country are attracted to us, to Freedom Road and now Liberation Road. Our trend, I think what we used to fight with people about back in the late '70s and early '80s and that now has received a lot less resistance . . . We were part of a current of leftists that centered white supremacy and white privilege in the struggle for socialism.

The sort of righteousness and supremacy of national liberation movements—whether they were bourgeois-led or not—we felt like those struggles against white supremacy were important in the struggle against capital. And that socialists of all stripes needed to identify that and recognize and support that. A lot of other forces were much more class-oriented or didn't want to see divisions in the class. So that's a little bit of a trend that I come out of.

I feel we've learned a lot from liberation forces among women, among queer and trans folk, among African American nationalist organizations. We've seen the importance of working with those forces as part of the struggle and not from the perspective of, "If it's not the class struggle, then we don't want it." I think our organization has tried to see the multifaceted layers of good movement-building. And yeah, I've been around too long, but I feel I've been in the right places. Not in the sense that I've chosen to be, but just that I've been in spaces where I could learn from folks not of our tendency, and that we as an organization have tried to learn from folks not of our particular tendency.

The other part of our line that I think is important is that a lot of other folks decided they should become a revolutionary party and struggle for power as a revolutionary party. We felt it was premature. A lot of work needs to be done to decide if you're a revolutionary party and none of the organizations out there have. And at least half of them, if not three-quarters of them, are gone now. And, you know, we're still in communication and dialogue with lots of them, including the Communist Party of the United States of America, because we see the value of forces meeting and discussing and talking. We're going to have our differences, but the differences between one hundred people over there and a hundred people over there is meaningless in the context of the struggle against empire. And so it's important that we start the dialogue. Where we can work together, we do. We're in conversation right now with some of the Black nationalist forces around some work around police—white supremacists and the police and military. And, you know, that is good stuff. And we'll take it wherever we can go and we'll try to figure out the lessons from that.

So that's the trend I come out of. Yeah, we're a fairly multinational organization with lots of roots, drawing from some of our alliances with and/or mergers with folks in the Chicano movement out in California, Arizona, the Midwest and Southwest area, a bunch of varied elements that are still around and kicking. We're getting younger. We have lots of young people coming in. And it's a growth process. I'm happy to be a part of it and still able to attend meetings and speak my mind. That's great.

MO

We've been talking for an hour and fifteen minutes and we certainly could keep talking. But I also want to respect your time and we could start winding down if you want. As well, although it's been a long time, I consider you a friend and a comrade. And if you want to have a conversation about dysphoria, we can do that.

PH

I would love to, actually. Yeah, I would love to.

Esteban Kelly

Esteban Kelly is a professional facilitator, a cofounder of AORTA (Anti-Oppression Resource & Training Alliance), and currently works as the Executive Director for the US Federation of Worker Cooperatives. His first and most substantial encounter with transformative justice was a decade spent organizing with Philly Stands Up, a collective that facilitated accountability processes with people who had perpetrated harm.

MAX FOX
Would you introduce yourself however you like?

ESTEBAN KELLY
Sure. My name is Esteban Kelly. I organize from my home in Southwest Philadelphia—but I should say I don't identify as a "community" organizer because I kind of come at organizing from a sideways angle. Some of that is weaving different movements together; some of it is as a facilitator or someone who's doing political education; some of it is as an organizer helping to build up some of the structures for the social solidarity economy, meaning foundational work to expand economic democracy. A lot of that is really rooted in helping people understand racial capitalism, and then understand what it is that we can do about it—not just like in an individual, "in my personal life" sort of way, but as actors who are agents of change, helping to shape the world that's going to be. I guess for the conversation today that's really rooted in some of this: the politics of abolition and transformative justice.

The relevant organizing piece to introduce is that I was one of the earliest members of a collective based in Philly called Philly Stands Up, which I joined at the very end of 2004, and was really active in for over a decade.

MF
So to begin, we're doing these interviews as a way of understanding what this concept of accountability is. I'm going to come back to it later, but just off the bat, in an abstract way, what does it mean to you?

EK
I think the smallest unit of accountability is the relationship. Sometimes it's just acknowledging that there's a relationship there. The deeper I go in thinking about this work, I'm starting to think that the smallest site of change in accountability is within the self. That when we expand it out, accountability is this kind of cluster of social support to get somebody to a place where they can hold themselves accountable or do the work. But there's only so much that people outside of yourself can do, at a certain point, so it is a relationship that facilitates self-transformation.

But the actual object is the self, not the relationship.

EK

Hmm. Well if we're thinking about just reducing it to the
instance of being held accountable or taking accountability,
then yes. But if you zoom out one click, accountability is
recognizing what the impact of that self-transformation
is and the need for that, so it usually starts as external, and
then the transformation happens internally, and then it's
a zoom out and an acknowledgement of your ties to a bunch
of social relationships.

MF

That's great. Can you say a little bit about your personal
background? How does where you come from influence your
political work?

EK

I was born in New York. My dad's the youngest of five, all
born and raised in Jamaica. My cousins were also born there.
Basically everyone older in the family was born and mostly
grew up back on the island. Even my older sister was born
in Jamaica—she's about ten years older than me—so the
generation kind of slices that way. That immigrant story shapes
a lot of my family story. I always think about that documentary
Life and Debt and the impact of the International Monetary
Fund, the World Bank, colonialism, structural adjustment, all of
those things, and how it shaped my existence. It helps me make
more sense of—there's so many parallels between the way I
organize within the left, within queer communities, not just
as political organizing; sometimes around pleasure and social
relationships and joy—and ways in which that is an exact echo
of what my dad was doing thirty, forty, almost fifty years ago.
I'm like, "Oh shit I truly am like the product of my parents."
They were doing the same thing within their community—the
Jamaican diaspora in New York. My dad knows all the goddamn
Jamaicans, he knows the people in the consulate office, he
knows the Jamaican taxi drivers. He would send them to pick
me up from the airport when he couldn't. I'm just like, "Oh cool
that 'super-connector' guy is my dad," and now that is what I

do—it's just in a completely different world.

I grew up on Long Island in a Jewish community. When I was born we lived in a lower-middle class community just outside of Brooklyn, like you could walk to Brooklyn from there, pretty close to JFK Airport. Then, when I was about three, my parents moved out to the suburbs into an upper-middle class community, but in a working class/lower-middle class neighborhood, which is where all the Puerto Ricans and Haitians and folks of color who were recent immigrants and who were either upwardly mobile or trying to be upwardly mobile had kind of established themselves in what was basically a liberal (Reform) Jewish community. So a lot of the Jewish families were upwardly mobile. I remember, growing up, I would talk with my friends' dads who grew up working class in Brooklyn but had become doctors, lawyers, finance, and businessmen. It was weird. Their kids, my peers, were a couple degrees removed from that working class struggle. Anyway, that's where I grew up. I went to a very bougie public school. Like, a few of my high school teachers had PhDs from Ivy League schools. My middle school chorus teacher was trained at Juilliard, his wife was a Rockette. He composed the new Russian national anthem . . . he had us perform at Lincoln Center with the Columbia Glee Club. It was a whole thing.

MF

That's incredible, thank you. So, when did you radicalize, or where do you locate that, because it sounds like you're going back over this personal trajectory, discovering that actually it was maybe there all along in certain ways. But there's always a kind of moment when you yourself . . .

EK

Interesting. Where do I locate the radicalization moment? I was always a critical thinker but I don't attribute my teenage radicalism purely to alienation and critical thinking. That alone might get you to a progressive, Elizabeth Warren set of politics. It does require a depth of getting connected to the left at a certain point, and of deeper critical thinking. For me that kind of catalyzed when I was in seventh grade. The opening for me was through punk music—part of that cultural wave in the nineties. It was just so helpful that the punk community was so easy to find and its politics so directly taught. You didn't have to jump through multiple steps to plug in. It was this discrete community. It was easy to go from DIY punk shows in someone's backyard or basement to doing Food Not Bombs and eventually being on the front lines of direct action.

I just remember being about fifteen years old, using my school-learned Spanish to speak with Salvadoran immigrants with Long Island Food Not Bombs. We were serving them meals, me and my more political punk friends, at the Long Island Railroad train station, and I was the only one in our group with real Spanish proficiency. And it wasn't difficult to continue my political development because I had really fucking smart "elders"—they were only like three or four years older than me—who were breaking down the difference between anarchy and anarchism and all these political traditions and introducing me to Marx. At that age it was easy to be politicized by just listening to bands like Propagandhi that were talking about the IMF and the World Bank and the World Trade Organization in their songs. I was making those connections to the Zapatistas, who were kind of popping off, to Noam Chomsky, a lot of that stuff. So for me it was less about having the itch for yearning for some progressive change and more around the meaning-making that my alienation started to fit into a framework or analysis of what the fuck was actually going on.

I didn't have access to a lot of the politics around Palestinian struggle, for example, given everything I just said about where I grew up. I went to Jewish summer camp for a couple years. I just wasn't even remotely exposed to that until college, until I was at UC Berkeley, and I was like, wait a minute, these are the people I agree with and it turns out there is a deeper story.

MF

Would you do a quick timeline of the things that you got involved with first, and then what were the kinds of things you threw yourself into? I know you got involved in co-op stuff at Berkeley—what are some orgs or campaigns . . .

EK

So when I was mentioning Food Not Bombs, we had a group called the Modern Times Collective and it kind of functioned through a spokescouncil model. We had a chapter of anti-

racist action, there was a women's collective, there was
an environmental justice collective, there was Food Not
Bombs, there was an anarchist reading group or whatever it
was—not just reading, there was a whole direct action/rapid
response flying squad . . . So the main center of gravity was
the collective, the Modern Times Collective, which organized
events, brought people in from the Independent Media Center—
from back when indie media stuff started happening—they
were bringing people in from there. They were really tight with
folks from Murray Bookchin's Institute for Social Ecology.
So I got connected with Brooke Lehman and Brad Will and
some of those folks when I was like fifteen. That's how I met
people from what became the political community around
Bluestockings and some of the anarchist info shops, even when
I was going to shows. Oh yeah, it was the fucking Wetlands! I
was going to ska shows and hardcore shows at the Wetlands,
which was a venue that was explicitly organized around this idea
of environmental justice, protecting the natural commons, and
understanding our relationship to that. They had pamphlets and
stuff floating around that venue. The culture back then, I have to
say, was strong. Of course, it was niche and the political range
was deeply self-limiting as an alternative subculture. But for all
my critiques around that, it also was really potent if you were
connected to it. It was not any of this surface-level aesthetic
mall culture that was also happening in the '90s, epitomized by
"posers." For us, if you were in it you were fucking in it. You
would be at a show and someone would get on the mic and give
you a fucking lecture for twenty minutes about whatever the
fuck shit was going around. Amadou Diallo, Matthew Shephard,
Bosnia, the virgin Redwoods . . . like I said, the IMF and the
Zapatistas. It was no fucking joke and I feel so grateful for it; I
just soaked it all up like a sponge.

   I had a job—one of my first paid organizing jobs—as a
peer educator in a "pride for youth" program. It was part of a
nonprofit, so I would be paid to table at events. Usually I would
be like, well, no one else from our queer youth program thing
is in these punk/hardcore/ska shows, so I'll be the guy at those
shows who's tabling and handing out free condoms and info
about safer sex, mental health, intimate partner violence or
whatever. But that was just part of it. It was just sort of like, oh,
someone who's visibly queer in this fucking dude-dominated,

white-dominated punk space. But people were tabling about shit all the time. It's just part of the culture space.

MF

Where does the Modern Times thing come from? Did they form out of a particular tendency or scene?

EK

Well, the same scene, a sort of anti-war and anarchist scene, and eventually that's how I got connected with Malav [Kanuga], through those same friends, but years later. By the time that Bluestockings stuff was happening I was already on the West Coast and he was in New Jersey; we eventually connected up when my Long Island people kind of melded in New York. Jersey was its own scene, in some ways it may as well have been California. But once you got past the teeny bopper anarchism, some of us were moving into . . . well, we were eighteen, nineteen, twenty years old. I had left for Berkeley around then, but that's where those organizing scenes started connecting. Malav and Team Colors, which included Craig Hughes and Kevin Van Meter . . . they did the *In the Middle of a Whirlwind* thing that Philly Stands Up contributed to.

MF

Oh, sure. Yeah.

EK

So that was sort of the crew at the time; it was a lot of Zinn, Chomsky, proper anarchists, and anarchist movements, Midnight Notes collective. That tendency. There was basically no viable communist party. I'm still really close with Kevin Van Meter. I fucking love him. In vampire lore, as an analogy, he would be the guy who sired me, he's the guy who bit my fucking neck, and was like, "Here. You need to know about the Midnight Notes collective, Silvia Federici . . . " All of that shit, it was them. And that's the tendency, really, when it comes down to it. There was a yawing generation gap between us and elders like Federici. They were the old, inviting elders. We were separated by fifty, sixty years. It was teenagers, and they were inviting card-carrying communists who were fifty years older than us to come talk to us and be like, "It's so wonderful that kids these days are interested in these tendencies," because the Gen X-ers were fucking nowhere to be seen, they were gone, didn't exist. Boomers skipped over them because they all became fucking liberals. So it was like they became the only fucking communists.

I mean, all elder anarchists were Bookchinites, because Midnight Notes . . . they were drawing on some of those elements and some of the Harry Cleaver that was here, so it was sort of there and not just background. We participated in solidarity and protest stuff together. Through Modern Times Collective, Kevin got us a school bus which we loaded up with Long Island kids and drove us down to Philly for a Mumia solidarity rally in like 1998, and that was my first time coming here other than for a punk show or on tour with my band.

MF

All the time you had this kind of organically political scene and then there were these moments that did properly political stuff that gave you whatever education.

EK

Well, there was militancy and it was like baby militancy, but it was there nonetheless, and there were ties to a movement and to elders. The internet was just emerging, you couldn't just Google who some of the Black Panthers were. It was even having a sense that this existed in the world. There was still a lot of aftershocks from COINTELPRO stuff coming, they were bombing Judi Bari and all the Earth Liberation Front (ELF) stuff, were charged by the FBI at the time as eco-terrorists and some of the members of Modern Times Collective were involved in some of those lawsuits. So anyway, that's where I came from, and then I fled New York. It was like, I need to get out of here, and when I showed up in California, I was like, "Oh I already know how to navigate this," which hippies to avoid, and how to find the ones who actually had some militancy going on there.

I got involved with the Commemoration Committee for the Black Panther Party that was based in Oakland and Berkeley at the time, and then, when I was at Berkeley, I was like, "Oh wait, you guys already have these cooperatives for social housing. Does anyone know about this? Why aren't you militant?" That was, for me, the beginning of connecting some of those dots.

MF

Where did your work with TJ, accountability, abolition stuff show up? How did you get involved with Philly Stands Up?

EK

I was recruited. I moved back to the East Coast, to Philly. I already had friends here, and they put me to work right away. They were like, "Here are the childcare shifts you're going to do for the movement parents who need child care." Some of that was for the parents involved in the sister or companion group to Philly Stands Up, called Philly's Pissed, which was a survivor support group. Both groups were new, they'd only been around for a couple months before I got to West Philly. So I was initially recruited to help because I was like, "I just got here. I'm new in town." And they were like, "Great, here's what you're doing." I was really confused about the difference at the time, but they were like, "There's a group called the Philly Dudes Collective, go to that." That was a collective of men who were committed to dismantling male supremacy and to understanding how it operated in our own lives and in the world. We designed popular education workshops on those themes for our community and sometimes at national summits like the National Conference on Organized Resistance (NCOR).

And concurrently there was another group called Philly Stands Up. The women I'm talking about were like, we want you to go to that too. With Philly Stands Up, a friend of mine was like, "I'm a survivor and I want you to be in that group on my behalf, to advocate and support me in the situation I was involved in." And then another person, someone who I knew even before moving to Philly was Cristy Road. Cristy and I first connected when I was in a touring band. I arrived in Philly and Cristy was living here. I subletted her room, actually, when I first got to town. She was involved in Philly's Pissed and was like, "Yeah I'm double-recruiting you." So I was hearing in stereo that I needed to be part of this group. Also I was like, this is a great way to meet people by helping and organizing, being involved in local things. So that's how I got involved initially, and it was auspicious timing because Philly Stands Up had just been founded in August of 2004 and I moved to town in November of 2004. When I moved to town it was like two weeks after a meeting.

MF

Do you know about the origin story of Philly Stands Up?

EK

There was a really stupid punk fest going on. No shade to the people who have matured since those times, but this punk fest . . . it was one of these goofy macho punk festivals (not political like the ones I referenced from my teenage years), where people—mostly crusty white dudes—came in from all over the country. During the festival that summer a series of sexual assaults took place at that event. And out of it, in response, a group emerged called Philly's Pissed as a circle of support for survivors of those sexual assaults, and then others beyond that. At the time it was women—I want to say all cis women—and they were like, "Cool, we're doing this thing." Then they organized the men to be like, "Y'all should get your shit together because this is not just about surviving, supporting our work." So they were kind of organized to form a men's group and they called it Philly Stands Up, which was an affiliate or companion group. It was initially founded by these punk, anarcho, cis men in response to the punk fest assaults. But it almost immediately became a vehicle for Philly cis dudes to show up and be like, "Look how antisexist I am by being publicly visible in this group."

So it had these meetings of like thirty or forty people, and then a couple of months go by and one after another after another, those dudes—which, obviously when there's like thirty or forty dudes from the punk scene all meeting, somebody's going to be called out for some shit. One after another they start getting called out for causing harm in sexual assault situations within our own community. That quickly snowballed into a crisis about what to do about it, because it was like, "Oh but these are guys who aren't low status, we're not willing to kick them out of town." They were like, "Oh shit, what do we do" when it's the people who are in the bands and booking the shows and are famous ("punk famous") and have all this clout and we're all homies and roommates with them?

And so, thank fucking god, two of the dudes stepped up (I imagine Philly Pissed had some influence on that) and were like, "Look, our next meeting is coming up in a couple weeks, and in that meeting our agenda is going to include addressing this situation, holding these folks accountable." And this is not a public show of feigned—what we currently call "virtue signaling." They called out these men in the group suggesting that they were "dealing with [their] male privilege" or whatever the language of the time was. They're like, "No, we're going to take this seriously. This is what's on the agenda, if you're not down, then don't come." So the group went from like thirty people to three at that following meeting. Only three guys showed up.

I moved to town two weeks after that disaster, was recruited into Philly Stands Up, and within a week or two, two other people were recruited into it. So I was part of a new group that was helping to restart it. One of my first meetings, it was like six people and I was like, "What's up with this? What are we doing? Hi guys, I'm new in town," and they're like, "This is our second meeting of licking our wounds and being like what are we actually doing and let's get serious now." In some ways, it was the beginning of us actually taking the work seriously; serious work wasn't happening until that point. I think I was the only person of color out of the six. One of the new people who was recruited was nonbinary and the two of us were hella queer and then over the course of that winter a bunch of the other cis guys were like, "Yeah, I'm kind of bisexual. I'm kind of exploring. I'm kind of . . . " So it starts unfolding, but overnight it shifted from being this punk cis white dude thing to becoming multiracial, multigendered, and a little bit gay, and taking the work seriously. I think that also coincided with . . . accountability actually scared all the dudes away, which in some ways needed to happen.

MF

It's like a controlled burn or something. Burn out all the dry brush. So what happened?

EK

There's some reason why they were the ones who were able to think resolutely about that and everyone else got freaked out . . . They had integrity. They had relationships, and they were like actual feminists. Juxtaposed with a bunch of dudes who in the original Philly Stands Up just wore pins saying, "I'm so antisexist, I'm innocent."

What went down was a showdown between shallowness and depth. Maybe some of it was more that some of the dudes hadn't thought that critically and didn't want to be seen as throwing their homie under the bus. There wasn't a politics of restorative justice [RJ] at the time, but you have to understand, this was just a group responding to a situation. There was no marquee politics behind it. There was a set of points of unity that I can't remember if they started drafting before the big diminishing or right around the time when I was running the group, but I know that when I showed up there was a set of points of unity, a living document. They were working on them, like, "Here's a page and a half of bullet points, read them, if you agree to them, then you can be in, if you have critiques of them, that's helpful. This is an opportunity for us to be in dialogue or to discuss those things and maybe amend them." And there was a point of unity that was like, "we are men responding to . . . " and we were like, "No, no, no—let's actually get out the red pen, let's talk about what it is that really matters about who we are and what we're doing." So I think that democratic deliberation element and that transparent and accountable element of knowing that it wasn't just like, here are the points of unity, just agree and get with the program, but rather a space to shape this thing . . . and this thing is open to grounded critique and response to that critique—that it was an invitation. It didn't feel like I had to like stick my nose out if I had constructive changes to offer . . . to be like, "You guys, you know as the only Black person in the group, as someone who is new in town . . . " But to know that my voice was invited and had everything to do with the trajectory that the group went through.

It took a few years, but probably three or four years into it, the group gradually shifted from being more in the punk community to being more in the queer community, to actually becoming a QTPOC-led group. It was queer, Jewish, Black, Puerto Rican. That's kind of who we are nowadays. There might be only one cis guy, I think, at this point in Philly Stands Up (me!). So it's had a full one-eighty, where I was the odd one out and now, well, I'm still very positive but with much more affinity, because I'm looking around, and I'm like, "K, there's other Black people, there's other immigrants, there's other Caribbeans, there's other queer people (all of us!)." Great movement, folks.

And, in fact, in the beginning, there really was not any engagement with theory. We got there at a certain point somewhere before leading up to the transition. We were still the punk group that was becoming more queer, but someone, the date of one of the members, was in a grad school or undergrad program, and they were like, "Oh I'm reading about this restorative justice thing and it kind of sounds like what you guys are doing, you should read up more about it." And we're like, "Let's go into study group mode and teach ourselves even just a taste of this thing called restorative justice."

It was less that we were studying it and learning how to do it, and more that it helped us understand what we were already doing. It was a full-on praxis—build the fucking road by walking. We fumbled our way through it, we made a kajillion mistakes, but we learned from all of the mistakes and we stuck around and we approached it with care. We didn't burn ourselves out and it was all about the way that we organize much more so than what it looked like externally. We met every Sunday. Every Sunday evening for a decade. We made meals for each other, we arranged childcare—it was somebody's job, like, "Who's the notetaker, who's facilitator, who is coordinating childcare?" Every fucking week. It taught me a lot about organizing.

I joined this club, I was like twenty-four years old, and I was like, "Oh that's part of organizing." You have to just make sure there's childcare for people, and if there isn't, that parent is just not gonna show up. They're like, "No, I'm not coming unless there's child care, it's not my job to arrange it myself." It seems so basic now (progress in our movements!), but back then it wasn't commonplace to organize that way. Community care and feminism had a long way to go. So everything about that set the right tone and I attribute our overall resilience to that, because other people working on this shit burned out in a fucking second. We had many minor brushes, including moments where . . . that moment in 2004 wasn't the first time that someone in the group was called out. It happened again and again. We moved through that process with integrity and people would step back or slide from one group to the other group. Some folks burned out on dealing with the people who caused harm, so they would just go to Philly's Pissed instead to support survivors. People were all over the place.

MF

This is great. You know, it's funny, you've actually moved through the questions I'm going to ask you. So, how did you come to start working on accountability in an informal way—were there informal practices that you used beforehand? How did they work? And then how did you first encounter the formal practice you just told the story about? I'm hearing some echoes from the punk scene lineage that that's what sort of brought these practices together to begin with. And you're saying you already had this kind of practice, some formal organizational structure with the spokescouncils and the tabling and education.

EK

Well, then when I got involved in the student co-ops—it's not just housing, but like, the Berkeley Student Co-op was massive and complex. We had 1,300 members who were basically as diverse (class, country of origin, ability, gender, race, religion, ethnicity, politics, you name it!). Jumping into that at eighteen or twenty years old was a master class in governance. I learned how to use Robert's Rules. These are kids who knew how to set up a detailed, efficient agenda. Keep in mind this was in a college setting, so there was high turnover, and we had to constantly train up the next generation of members to continue stewarding this multimillion-dollar social enterprise, which had already been around for seventy years back then. So I knew how to orient and train new people into doing that shit. I mean, these are people organizing what is sort of like the logistics that go into an Amazon warehouse, but like, the student version of that. You had a warehouse and we were doing hundreds of thousands of dollars of food purchasing and delivery to twenty-three properties which we owned. My first work-shift job involved driving a truck on a delivery route to all those houses and apartments. All these buildings needed major maintenance. It was like, how do we pass a city kitchen health board inspection? It was complex. There were negotiations to lease land from the University of California. There were huge social challenges—sexual assaults, suicides, and drug overdoses. We employed like twenty-five professionals but otherwise, there were no grown-ups, it was us. So yeah, jumping into all that, with the background I already had, it gave me a super skillset in how to organize.

MF

And that's kind of what you brought into this. How would you describe that politically? Are those just organizing skills that are common to many different movements or . . . ?

EK

Yeah, well, maybe I'll take that back. I don't think I brought that to Philly Stands Up. I feel like there was a sense in which I brought that to some of the organizing happening in the Cedar Park community in West Philly. I immediately found myself immersed in all these different elements that the Movement for a New Society had created back in the '70s and '80s. They set up all these solidarity and cooperative institutions that were all deteriorating by the early 2000s. It was such a contrast to Berkeley. They had these institutions set up and people trying to run them without training or practice (with the notable exception of Training for Change, which does facilitation stuff). These things were not grounded in methodology, in rigor, in the context of what it meant to be like, "Why do we do things by consensus?" "I don't know, that's how it's always been." "Has anyone been trained in using consensus?" "Like, one and a half fucking people." So I did bring that to the Life Center Association (LCA) land trust which I lived in for a dozen years, to Mariposa Food Co-op, which I staffed for close to a decade back when it was worker-managed, some of the other Movement for a New Society institutions. I wasn't that involved in the A-Space other than living above it and occasionally organizing some events, supporting Books Through Bars— some of the other pieces of it.

Anyway, jumping back to Philly Stands Up . . . It was not really set up as a formal institution. It was never incorporated. It was all below the radar, which was really helpful. It meant we never needed liability insurance. It meant when people who we were trying to hold accountable for harm were like, "I'm gonna sue you," we were like, "Well, we're not a thing per se, who are you gonna sue? You only know my punk name. You don't even know who the fuck we are." Which cuts both ways, often.

We would get cease and desist orders for what we were doing. There were people who . . . we were like, "Hi, we're here to work with you because of a situation." And often, I don't know, maybe 25 percent of the time, they would just be like, "No, thank you." It was ultimate panic—male panic, male fragility stuff. They were like, "If you come after me that's libel and my reputation is my livelihood because I do such and such touring art or music or whatever," or, "If you tarnish my reputation . . ." We would get letters from like— look, because these are upper-middle class white guys by and large—they would be like, "Talk to my lawyer." A lot of the ones who would push back with liaison stuff were the middle class ones. So we would often encounter that, and had a whole protocol—again, all of which we just figured out by fucking doing it. We were not connected to any of this national stuff which we didn't always even know was happening. I mean, we knew sexual assaults were happening, we knew the punk community, but we didn't—.

MF

What did you think? There was no one to learn from? What was the thing you thought you were doing? "We are this body that's addressing this problem that is called sexual assault?"

EK

Yeah, it came down to the points of unity. We had a lot of stuff, like, we never fucking call the police, we always believe survivors, we don't fuck with the legal system. It wasn't because we were self-aware abolitionists per se . . . I mean, we were abolitionists but we weren't using that language. It wasn't from a principle, it wasn't grandiose, because we're working at a small scale. We were like, "Well this is what makes sense." Initially, because we were accountable to Philly's Pissed, it was set up hierarchically. Like, they were the group that was in charge and we were accountable. There was a lot of tension over the course of our evolution to being like, "Actually, we can't," just because sometimes they would say, "Now we're gonna do a smear campaign against this person who's caused harm because they're not working with you," and we're like, "Actually that's not in the well-being of our community comprehensively, as a whole." Or they would say, "We're gonna go beat this person up," and we'd be like, "Could you not actually? We're gonna tell you that you shouldn't," and they're like, "But we have to center survivors," and we're like, "Yeah, the more we do this work, the more we think it's more complicated." We had to stumble into and discover this politics of restorative and transformative justice, and it's why it made so much sense when we finally got connected to that broader TJ community. It was like we already had all this wisdom from praxis, because we had been doing it for five, six, seven years before we even heard a whisper of the term "transformative justice." And then we start connecting to Generation FIVE and to like all the queer organizers and women of color and a lot of folks connected to INCITE! and the Allied Media Conference world. I really attribute it to a lot of the survivors of color, women of color, who came and found us.

We were just a bunch of twenty-somethings, well actually at the time, we went through iterations, but by the time we connected with more national stuff we were mostly in our twenties and early thirties. When I first joined, there were parents who were already in their thirties, maybe even early forties, so it already was a little . . . I wouldn't say multigenerational, but our age-range spanned fifteen, twenty years. But by the time we got pulled into this, I was suddenly the oldest person in the collective and we just sort of saw ourselves as kids who were pretty humble. We just stumbled our way into this stuff and we kept waiting for other people to be proposing training sessions and be able to engage in dialogue, waiting for someone else to take the lead. And it just wasn't happening. So finally we were like, "I don't know, this US Social Forum thing is happening, should we submit a session?" And then we did, and we were like . . . "I guess!" And next thing I know, Mimi Kim and Leah Lakshmi Piepzna-Samarasinha show up to our Social Forum workshop and are sitting right in the front row. We got organized by them and there's so much grace with which . . . I can't imagine their patience, because I must have been such a fucking mess, such a novice . . . I was in my twenties and just didn't know what the fuck was going on in a wider TJ community of practice . . . I didn't have context around all the other things.

We knew how to hold dialogue with people who caused harm. We knew how to share some of our lessons, some of

the challenges around this work, but there was no reason
it should have been us in the front of the room rather than
people from the Bay Area Transformative Justice Collective
or Creative Interventions. But that's how we met all those
folks, like Mimi Kim, Mia Mingus, Ejeris Dixon. So yeah, we
put on this session in Detroit at the US Social Forum and got
one of these gigantic rooms, and there were like hundreds
of people in our fucking workshop, and we were like, "What
is happening?!" And then it turned out that all the people
were like, "We've been following what you've been doing."
We're like, "What? How do you even know?" "Oh you put
out some zines and you've done some workshops, like little
conferences here and there," and we're like, "Yeah, but . . .
what?" So a lot of the people who are involved in that came to
that workshop, then they lingered afterwards and were like,
"OK, you now need to be brought into this whole community
of queer folks of color who are much deeper in this work."
And yet they still felt like they had a lot to learn from us. They
thought the difference was we had not professionalized it,
that was a major difference. They all either had like one toe in
academia or nonprofits. It was like the Audre Lorde Project's
Safe OUTside the System (SOS), Community United Against
Violence (CUAV) in San Francisco. It turned out to be a wide
web. The Young Women's Empowerment Project in Chicago,
all of those kinds of groups. The good side of that is they had
access to resources. So folks from the Audre Lorde Project
had gotten a grant to have a convening, invite-only, of QTPOC
who were working on this. People like Cara Page from
Healing Justice, a lot of disability justice organizers, and they
were like, "We got a hotel in Miami, off season. It's got a hot
tub and we're all gonna get together, learn from each other,
chill, build relationships." We were all out and they were like,
"You guys should be there." I was like, "OK, well you should
send some of the femmes from Philly Stands Up." And they
were like, "No, Esteban, you are coming."

I was like, "Really?" And they're like, "Yes." So they just
organized the shit out of me—that was three months after that
workshop in Detroit. They had a grant to do that. So they flew
everyone into Miami and we built relationships. And then we
were like, "Oh, OK, I guess we are peers with these people who
were developing this concept."

And you continued doing the same work or you started
changing some of the stuff you had started?

EK

We started working on fewer and fewer situations and doing
more and more political education and really helping to
nurture or foment the . . . I want to say movement but like,
this network around transformative justice. And wow, this
was all around the same time. So June 2010 was the Social
Forum, August was that retreat. In January 2011 Philly Stands
Up organized a transformative justice action camp in Philly.
For all of its problems and stuff, we really just thought—we're
hearing from all these young new graduates or college kids
or just queer organizers who were like, "Let's come together,
it's gonna be this popular education thing, we're gonna
introduce these models, learn from each other, it's really
introductory." We posted registration online. We had people
from Generation FIVE, people who had written and coined the
term "transformative justice," all the people. I mentioned there
was Mimi Kim, Leah Lakshmi Piepzna-Samarasinha, Kiyomi
Fujikawa, RJ Maccani, all those folks. And we were like, "Oh,
this is becoming a different thing than what we originally
thought it was gonna be." So clearly there's still a need and this
was the second time we had kind of stumbled into organizing
the thing that needed to happen even though we were the babies.

Why wasn't there a session at the US fucking Social
Forum in 2010 proposed by anyone else? I don't know why. I
mean the Social Forum . . . there was Atlanta in 2007, then there
was Detroit in 2010. I mean, that was it like, OK, I'm sure there
were sessions at the Allied Media Conference, but anyway.

So that was January 2011. We did it over MLK weekend,
so I remember that, and we deepened a lot of relationships,
really sank into that. That was where it really got rigorous, and
thank god it wasn't like an intro, because we got to all learn
and we just were like here are the things that are tensions,
here's what's problematic, here's where we are running into
walls, what do we do around . . . How much are we centering a
politics of abolition versus kind of doggedly pursuing whatever
the survivor says? How do we expand our understandings of
a community of survivors? That intimate partner violence

affects everyone? We're really zooming out and considering TJ
and then linking it to things like community violence, linking
it to starting to talk, even back in 2011, about the co-optation
of RJ into school programs, alternative schools, all of that shit.
Anyway, it was wonderful, and that's why I'm friends with these
people, because they came and found me and we organized. And
Philly Stands Up, we kept threatening to—we were like, "Hey, I
think this collective, I think it's done, people are moving away,
we're shifting our attention to other things," and all these folks
from the movement were just like, "No, it brings tears to my
eyes, the idea of PSU shutting down," and we're like, "OK, well
we're gonna go 'emeritus mode,' we're just gonna keep it on life
support." We're semi-retired, we'll be around to have a retreat
every couple years.

And actually the last time we had a retreat was on MLK
Day January 2020, right before the pandemic. It was a mini
reunion. It's the last time I touched all those people and then
the next summer was like the kind of national uprising—six
months later, five months later, everything popped off.

MF

I'm hearing that you guys kind of organically developed these
concepts because you were sort of stumbling your way towards
the processes that were necessary for these situations you were
tasked with responding to, and then you found this formal
level that they existed on. Did you then revise your idea of the
history of these ideas? Like—these people have been the kind
of caretakers of a tradition that we spontaneously discovered on
our own, or they've invented it here in the Bay and now we're
kind of joining and diffusing it with our stuff?

EK

I think we always were really aware, because we did our fucking
homework, so we were aware of a lot of First Nation and
Indigenous practices around RJ. We were just like, "Oh this is
how humans have survived on Earth before colonialism." So
we often would put that in the context of any of our workshops
about it, film screenings, whatever. So we were aware of
that deeper history, I think mostly from movement people
who pursued that history, that lineage, much more closely
and rigorously. From what we hear, restorative justice was

always couched as, or bracketed as, or framed as applying to everything except sexual assault and maybe murder. I think it was just rape and murder. So it's like, theft and lies and whatever, maybe even kidnapping.

So we were like, "Oh that's part of what's different about this term," that it's not around the very cyclical and circular idea of restoration and harmony and repair that comes from Indigenous cultures, but that in a lot of ways it is and it's embedded in the Western late capitalist social relationships we find ourselves embedded in. That there is something that's historically particular to what it is that we're doing, because when we talk about transformation, we're talking about engaging with all of the social relationships that are wrapped up in racial capitalism. And those are the things that need to be transformed, ultimately, when we talk about white supremacy, heteropatriarchy, and its particular formations in our lives. From the moment theft is the crime, it's like—well what even is ownership? What even is right?

So transformative justice is begging all of those questions by decentering this punitive vilifying thing, where you're the one who's the villain, and then inviting in what I was starting to say around the importance of relationship and getting outside of all these diametrical relationships and being like, no, we are part of a web of relationships. And so again, we stumbled into that by working with people and learning the hard way, being like, "This person isn't in a place to take accountability or be accountable because they're having a mental health crisis, they're houseless, they have an addiction problem, they don't have a job." So we were like, "Oh, let's get you therapy referrals, let's get you a stipend for transit or food, let's help you find a house," like basic fucking things. "Let's make sure that there's someone in your life who hasn't disposed of you and still has trust where you can feel that relationship."

People really forget to even have a shred of empathy for someone, forget about whether or not it happened, whether or not they're quote unquote "guilty," for someone who is in the crosshairs of being called out, period. It fucking sucks. And when you sit down with multiple of those people every month, it starts to become really clear. Like, if my end goal is you taking accountability, we gotta back all the way up. And the conversation included Philly's Pissed back in the day, before they dissolved that collective and were reborn in the modern era as the affiliate survivor support collective, because they're like, "Oh our politics have changed."

It became really clear that you can't start with accountability; accountability is way far down the line, so many steps later from like—are you capable of even showing up to a conversation? And mind you, this is what it would look like: we would be sitting often in a neutral open public space—we weren't like sitting on my couch—to have the conversation, see where the person is at, and have them talk, share, reflect, and eventually open up their ability to listen.

It was before any of us were really deep in any of these clinical methodologies like cognitive behavioral therapy or any of this. We were just doing it because there's a truth behind it, and so you're just gonna stumble upon it if you're pursuing the truth; it will lead you to that place. So with folks we worked with, no one would explicitly say you need to be on time or communicate about it. When you don't do that that's violating a boundary. So that this is a practice of, or an exercise in, practicing what it looks like to communicate, to be accountable, to uphold those boundaries and respect other people. This isn't even sexualized, it's like—can you get your shit together? Can you communicate? Can you communicate, including when there's something that's hard to say? Like, "Oh yeah, I didn't do the reading. You told me to read this bell hooks article." Like, just fucking be honest, let's be vulnerable, let's practice that. There weren't any other spaces or people to do that in our community. So that's what Philly Stands Up really was, it was just a space to test that out.

Creating a space to practice those things, including for ourselves, for the community to have an organ or an appendix that was actually doing that, and then we ended up learning all these lessons from that. We were like, "We can't just keep this to ourselves just because we're working at this small scale." We need to weave this into some political education and let our community know all this stuff that we're finding, and then we hitched it to the things we're learning about transformative justice.

MF

That's so amazing. I have so many more questions but I kind of want to stop there if that's alright.

Emi Kane & Hyejin Shim

Emi Kane has been an activist and organizer since she was a teenager, particularly in the New York chapter and later the National Organizing Collective for INCITE! (formerly INCITE! Women of Color Against Violence) for almost ten years.

Hyejin Shim has similarly done anti-violence work with survivors of sexual violence for a decade, including with the California chapter of Survived & Punished, of which she is a national cofounder.

M. E. O'BRIEN

Let's start off with both of you introducing yourselves.

EMI KANE

Both of you know me, but for the purposes of the interview, my name is Emi. She/her pronouns. I guess what's relevant to this conversation is that I was on the National Organizing Collective for INCITE!, formerly INCITE! Women of Color Against Violence, and have been involved with anti-violence organizing in various formations for decades.

HYEJIN SHIM

My name is Hyejin. I use she/her pronouns. I've been working with survivors of gender-based violence for the last decade or so, as a direct service provider and as an organizer. I am a member of the California chapter of Survived & Punished, and I am a cofounder of the organization as a whole.

MO

Excellent. I hope you both can share a lot more about your organizations' histories. So the umbrella concept that we're working with in these interviews is around accountability and the complexities and contradictions and what that means to people, how ideas about it have changed over time, and how it relates to other ideas. To start off, what does that word mean to you?

HS

To me, accountability means being responsible for your impact. This includes taking responsibility for harm you've caused, making amends where it's possible, and working to not repeat that same harm again.

EK

I think the term "accountability" can mean different things depending on the context and in some cases has been stripped of its meaning. When it comes to serious harm, abuse, or violence I think it means not just an apology, but being able to meaningfully demonstrate through your actions a commitment to changed behavior that will ensure that it doesn't happen again. I think accountability also means considering the impact

of your choices on your community and yourself, and accepting
the consequences of those choices.

MO

I want to strongly encourage you to reply to each other any time,
both with thoughts that come to mind, but also with questions
for each other. I find the best interviews are when people start
rambling and saying something new, saying something different,
and working it out as they're speaking. You mentioned the word
being stripped of meaning. Could you say more about that?

EK

Hyejin and I have talked a little about this, but I do feel like it's
thrown around a lot in ways that are not helpful. There isn't
always a clear expectation for what accountability might look
like, and there can be a lot of defensiveness when there's any
inquiry into that. I don't know, Hyejin, since we can make
this a dialogue, I feel like this is something that happens a lot,
in particular on social media. I think of this association with
accountability processes for violence or abuse, and it has
become ... maybe not stripped of meaning, but it's endowed
with meaning that it doesn't actually deserve, and then it can
be weaponized.

HS

I do think it's become a buzzword, and the meaning changes
depending on the person. I don't really think that there is a
universally agreed upon definition of accountability in practice.
It's hard to find public examples of accountability that don't
swing into the territory of meaningless buzzwords, like a sort of
complicity with violence. Or alternatively, that doesn't weaponize
the term in a way that is very disingenuous or harmful itself.
I have definitely seen domestic violence survivors be accused
of being abusive themselves, and then have accountability
processes used against them as another tool of harm and control.

EK

Yeah. I agree. I can speak from my own experience, and maybe
we'll get into that later. But because there's no real specificity
or shared understanding about what that term might mean, we
have situations where someone is asking for accountability,

often a survivor of some sort of violence that person is asking for accountability, and people project their own punitive expectations or values onto that term. So if somebody is saying, "Yes, I'd like accountability for harm or abuse or violence," and what they might really mean is, "I just don't want this to ever happen to another person." People hear the word accountability and make assumptions. Is there another word we can use? In dominant culture, we associate that term with punishment. Many people have internalized these carceral, punitive logics. It's like you're speaking another language, trying to explain to somebody, "No, I don't want punishment. I actually care about this person. And I would like something to happen so that this cycle of harm is interrupted." Sometimes it doesn't really matter what accountability means to the person who's calling for it, because it just gets so distorted and projected upon and turned into this ask for punishment, when it's often not.

I want to acknowledge that there may also be anger and a desire for revenge on the part of a survivor, which I personally think is healthy and valid in the face of violence. I would love to see more space made for people to feel angry about the violence they've endured. We seem able to make room for that when it comes to what we see as state and structural violence, but we often don't connect the dots and allow survivors the same space for anger when it comes to what we see as interpersonal violence—which by the way is not actually separate from state and structural violence. Anyhow, I almost never see people use asks for accountability as a way to act on that anger. Almost always, the ask for accountability is driven by desperation after many attempts at other, more private, approaches have been made and failed, and they usually revolve around a core concern: "I just don't want this to ever happen to another person. What can we do to figure out a way to prevent this from happening again? I went through it, I don't want it to happen to anyone else."

MO

Tell me about INCITE! and Survived & Punished and how they relate to these questions.

EK

INCITE! is at this point a fairly well-known collective. INCITE! was founded officially in the year 2000 at a conference called

The Color of Violence, which took place at UC Santa Cruz. And forgive me INCITE! folks if I'm misrepresenting INCITE! right now, but I wasn't at that conference. I knew about it at the time and was living in San Francisco but wasn't able to make it. It was called for essentially by—I'm going to use the terms that were used at the time—women of color who were organizing in several movements: anti–law enforcement violence, or at the time called it anti–police brutality organizing spaces, and as well women of color who had been sort of coming up through what in the '80s and '90s was called the Battered Women's Movement, and also just doing anti–domestic violence and sexual assault work. On the one hand, there was the anti–police brutality organizing spaces in which I think a lot of the women of color there were frustrated about a lack of gender analysis when talking about state violence. And then, on the other hand, when talking about interpersonal violence in the anti–domestic violence and sexual assault spaces, the lack of a racial justice analysis and a dominance of white carceral feminist frameworks that guided the practices in those spaces. There was also a concern that there was a lack of analysis that included both a connection between interpersonal and state violence and that there was even really a distinction between those. There is obviously a distinction in the way that it impacts people, but also in the analysis that there was a real disconnect. And so women of color from these movement spaces came together to create what became a collective called INCITE!. INCITE! was never a 501(c)3 nonprofit organization. It was a collective that I guess still exists, but I'm going to speak about it in the past tense for now.

As a collective, it operated with a national organizing collective, which I was a part of for quite some time. The national organizing collective helped to facilitate the movement of resources, merch, t-shirts, books, to help release statements, organize conferences, and publish books. And then there were chapters and affiliates. Affiliates were existing organizations or collectives—whether they were 501(c)3 nonprofit organizations or not, and for the most part they were not—who were allied with INCITE!'s work and then were brought into the network. And chapters were just sort of autonomous individual groups that usually operated as collectives in different cities around the country, doing anti-violence work through this lens. Most of

it took place in the United States. I think there was a Navajo or
Diné organization, which we considered not in the United States.
And then there were some campaigns that were taking place
outside of the United States and some in Canada as well. So that's
INCITE!. And there are going to be different perspectives on
this. My perspective is that the national organizing collective and
INCITE! itself functioned as a place where we could build shared
analysis and do political education. And I do think that INCITE!
was really effective at doing that. I think it was an integral part
of movement building and convening and developing projects,
and certainly most of us were involved with other kinds of
organizing. INCITE! also partnered with different groups like
Critical Resistance and others to build shared analysis across
different movement spaces and conversations.

MO

Why do you speak about INCITE! in the past tense? What
happened?

EK

I just don't think that INCITE! is organizing public campaigns
right now. There have been a couple of great events, like a
discussion with Angela Davis and Andrea Ritchie, and then an
event with INCITE! national collective members that took
place at the Barnard Center for Research on Women, maybe
a year ago. That felt like a little INCITE! reunion and was held
for the twentieth anniversary of the collective. A lot of that
energy seems to have carried over to Survived & Punished,
Interrupting Criminalization, Creative Interventions, and
other groups with INCITE! collective members doing similar
work. I was part of the early days of Survived & Punished,
and brought some former INCITE! folks to the table there.

MO

Hyejin, can you tell us about Survived & Punished?

HS

Sure, I think Survived & Punished is pretty directly in the lineage
of INCITE! because most of us met at INCITE!'s fourth
conference. The organizers for Marissa Alexander's campaign
were facilitating a workshop about defense campaigns, about their

strategies and lessons learned. Marissa's campaign was the only campaign I'd seen done for a criminalized survivor of domestic violence, specifically. I attended that workshop as someone who was, at the time, leading a survivor defense campaign for the first time ever—the Stand with Nan-Hui (SWNH) campaign. Emi and I actually first became friends through SWNH.

After that, SWNH connected with the Free Marissa Now organizers, California Coalition for Women Prisoners, and the Chicago Alliance to Free Marissa Alexander, which is now known as Love & Protect. We decided to come together to create a new national project, Survived & Punished, as a result of our conversations together. We saw there were so many parallels and similarities between cases, but there was no place where resources, shared lessons, and advocacy were centralized.

MO

What was compelling about INCITE!'s conference and framework and thinking for your vision?

HS

INCITE! was the only organization of its kind I knew of, and it had had a huge impact on me back when I was just starting to organize as a young person. Their work was very influential to my thinking, particularly on feminism and prison abolition. I went to that conference specifically because of the SWNH campaign, to find people who would be supportive. I thought, who would be supportive of this, and who will actually help out and spread the word? And this conference was coming up, so it felt like the right time and place.

EK

Can I add, there was a mini-conference that we co-organized at UC Berkeley after the INCITE! conference. It was the very first Survived & Punished public event. I remember at the very tail-end of SWNH, we had questions about what to do with the momentum and energy around the campaign, and I said, "My friend Alisa [Bierria] works at UC Berkeley Center for Race and Gender" (she also worked on the Free Marissa campaign). Maybe she'd let us do something there where we can bring together others who are working on freedom campaigns for criminalized survivors to talk about overlaps and next steps, or to form some sort of larger national coalition to continue this work. And then we did that. Alisa brought Renata Hill, one of the New Jersey Four, and we had a film screening, along with discussions and strategy sessions. I think Survived & Punished really coalesced around Color of Violence 4 (COV4) and that UC Berkeley convening, and it included some former INCITE! people. I still remember a discussion around that time about the name, and the hashtag for Twitter. I suggested Survived+Punished to save character space but we went with SurvivedandPunished, which is funny to think about now.

MO

Emi, you spoke a little bit about the sort of framework of thinking about violence that INCITE! was pushing back against—the lack of gendered analysis in the anti–police brutality movement, the carceral white feminist politics wrapped up with the Battered Women's Movement. What were the frameworks that INCITE! was drawing from or that were shaping your thinking or the thinking of other people early on in the process?

EK

I wasn't part of those conversations. I probably joined an INCITE! chapter in 2004, something like that. And I joined the national collective in 2007, so I was not around for those early conversations. Frameworks . . . I think people were speaking from their experiences, women of color who were trying to support women of color and immigrant survivors through, say, the shelter system. Again, maybe Hyejin can speak more to this, because that has been your paid work experience. I'm not sure what you're asking in terms of frameworks, but I think people were coming from a practical place. People were saying: We're building these campaigns, we're building frameworks or building practices around a particular type of subject or victim or survivor on all sides of these conversations. So in terms of law enforcement violence, a lot of the public messaging and more visible organizing was happening around the assumption that the survivor of police violence is usually a man of color, and what was left out of that was the experience of women of color who were just as often brutalized and harmed, killed, or assaulted by law enforcement. There was also a lack of analysis about law enforcement violence and military violence against women of color outside of the United States. So these are people who were speaking from their lived experience. And then, on the other side of the conversation it really was just about finding that, speaking, pushing back against the limitations of the resources that were available to women of color who were survivors. And the reliance on law enforcement and the criminal legal system as the main avenues of recourse for care for survivors of violence. I wasn't there for the very early conversations, though. Hyejin I think you can speak to some of that, too, not because you were there but because of your relationship to this aspect of the issue.

MO

Yeah. Where were people coming from? What do you think shaped people's political thinking that enabled them to do the thinking together in INCITE!?

HS

I can't speak to what was going on with INCITE! since I wasn't a part of it, but from my standpoint, they were the most visible entity that was explicitly rejecting both the criminal legal system's abuses as well as patriarchy and gender-based violence within communities of color and movement communities. I think they helped really make that clear for so many people. They articulated that constant tension that many survivors of color are experiencing, mediating, navigating constantly, which is how to survive violence without putting other people in harm's way, either violence from the state or from community members . . .

MO

It's very interesting that your answer is really emphasizing how the thinking emerges out of life experience and practical questions; that makes sense. And obviously that's true. A lot of different kinds of politics emerge out of life experience. Serious political thinking almost always requires engagement with both life experience and drawing on political frameworks, political thinking, political analysis that came before. And I mean, certainly, the prison abolition movement has a lot of complex roots in the histories of Black nationalism and Black socialist thought and revolutionary anarchist thought. And these evolved in conversations over the course of decades. And like, both of you weren't around for the initial conversations, but we are formed politically by not just immediate, practical life experience, because some people engage in practical struggles without developing a lot of political frameworks out of that. But it's in this sort of encounter and dialogue with revolutionary thought of a wide variety of sorts that people develop these kinds of analyses. For the frameworks that were used in the thinking you were doing: Where did it come from? What were its origins? What was its history? One answer, and obviously a very important part of it, was out of the life experience of women of color in these two movements. I'm asking if there's other dimensions of that that have to do with political ways of thinking about the world.

HS

I mentioned it earlier, but Survived & Punished is in the direct lineage of INCITE!. We really built upon that. And of course, several of us had been a part of INCITE! previously, also. But there is also a longer history of defense campaigns for survivors that came before. And our work draws from that.

In terms of us and our political frameworks, I think we are probably across the map, whether communist or anarchist. We draw from a lot of more informal and formal places too, as well as things that may not be explicitly labeled as Marxism or anarchism. I personally have been influenced by Marxist thinking, particularly in Marxist feminism, as well as the anarchist tendencies of the local queer/trans and activist spaces of the Bay Area. But it isn't so discrete or clear-cut. Many people are coming to this type of immediate survival work out of urgency, necessity, or the feeling that something is deeply wrong with this, and their politics are in different stages of articulation. I don't think that people always "end up" with a fully formed, traditional kind of understanding of ideology or framework, either, for better or for worse.

EK

Yeah, I think, again, similar to Hyejin, I'm not going to have the answer you probably want. Some of the people who were involved in INCITE! early on maybe brought some of those kinds of allegiances into the space, but honestly, I will speak from my own experience, most of the organizing I've done, that I learned from . . . Part of it is also being politicized through my own family experience, my family's experience, where there are people who would not identify as communist, anti-imperialists, feminists even, but they're teaching me those practices through their choices and actions.

MO

Hyejin, can you say more about the framework that leads people to really prioritize defense campaigns as a core part of their organizing over the course of many years? How did you get into defense campaign work and why did you stay with it?

HS

I got into defense campaign work because I was working at a domestic violence shelter at the time and was approached with a local case of a Korean immigrant criminalized survivor. The Korean community can be pretty tight-knit, and at the time I was part of this small Korean domestic violence collective of volunteers. Someone had reached out to us about this case. At that point, there were really no Korean-specific domestic violence resources left in the Bay Area for a number of reasons, including gentrification. So we, as a small group of people, brought our networks in to try to create a campaign, though none of us had ever done it before. We were just like, "Well, OK, let's do what we can."

So I was involved, both in a personal and professional capacity. I didn't want to take this case on strictly as an advocate-client relationship, with a more rigid nonprofit approach to it. It seemed like what was most necessary wasn't necessarily that type of formalized, more private relationship behind the scenes—but a broader public campaign, because the situation was in such a dire place. And again, Marissa Alexander's case was the model that we really looked to. The organizers of that campaign had also included several members of INCITE! like Alisa Bierria and Mariame Kaba.

With the defense campaign, what really grounded our thinking, our analysis, was what folks in INCITE! and immigration and abolitionist organizing had been putting out around: there are no perfect victims. A lot of what you see, especially in immigrant rights organizing, is this rhetoric of "so-and-so is not a criminal. Immigrants are not criminals." But the fact is that most, if not all, deportations begin with an arrest. By police. You become eligible for deportation through the process of criminalization, so actually, the immigrants who are being detained and deported are technically criminals. Criminal means nothing except that you've been criminalized by the state, and accepting its judgments while challenging, say, an individual charge or conviction is a slippery slope. There's always this lure towards exceptionalizing people with this idea that they're just innocent people so they don't deserve it. And that is harmful towards solidarity because you're saying that if you have been found guilty of a crime, then you deserve the violence of the state. So we wanted to be cautious about that, about the allure of trying to distance ourselves from the "bad" immigrants, "bad" survivors.

What kept me going was that this felt like such an important site to make interventions because policing, prosecution, and prisons are constantly justified in the name of protecting victims of violence. What about these people who were very much being punished, not protected, by the state? With how district attorneys and anti-violence organizations responded to such survivors, we really saw firsthand the ways that crisis response to gender violence is very deeply connected to policing. People feel as if policing is the only solution, to the point where many domestic violence and sexual assault agencies may feel like they have a symbiotic relationship with the police. I kept going because this felt like an area of work in which I had a lot of skills and interest, where we could make really concrete differences in peoples' lives. It was also to make these critical connections more visible, for this population of survivors that were very often forgotten or unseen. I also think it was exciting to figure out a way to anchor a gender analysis more into abolitionist organizing, because the two are not necessarily thought of by many as intersecting.

MO

That's very interesting. Emi, you mention there being multiple strands coming into the organization, or people coming from multiple, different places. Is that possible to talk about at all, the sort of the variety of different kinds of backgrounds that INCITE! brought together?

I think what I was trying to say with that is that the criteria for INCITE! was really that we all agreed on the same principles of unity and agreed to the statement of solidarity with Palestine, which we all know is more polarizing than it should be. But even among radicals, it was not something we could take for granted. So because of that, and because we did, a lot of people came to INCITE! through their experience rather than because of any sort of organizational allegiance. We had people from all over the map—all over the political map, all over the geographic map. Because of that, we were not a monolith. And that's always the case. But I think part of the reason for me, at least, that INCITE! was such a constructive space and also, I think, a project through which a lot of meaningful analysis was produced, is because we were working those things out in real time among ourselves and the group as a whole didn't have any narrow allegiance to any one framework. I think we were just working things out together in real time, so it was a really dynamic space and people were coming from all over the map. That's what I'll say. I don't know if that's helpful.

When I started organizing with the Nan-Hui Jo campaign, a lot of the people who first jumped on board were from the queer and trans left Korean community I had organized with for years. That was the result of a long time of building relationships together, as people who'd been thinking for a long time about things like diaspora politics, imperialism, and gender, for example. But this particular campaign was very direct and immediate. We needed to figure out our strategy, get people out, and keep adapting. When you're doing a defense campaign, timelines and conditions can change within a day or even within an hour. Some meetings we'd be planning for a court date or something the next week, and then we'd find out, during that meeting, that sentencing or something had been delayed again. So it was constantly shifting; it was just go, go, go. For SWNH we had alignment on being in solidarity with other defense campaigns and criminalized survivors, but it was all very practical, and not necessarily oriented around more typical understandings of political ideology. That had a lot to do with how much more immediate it was. Not all defense campaigns are so time-sensitive, because it depends on the stage of someone's case, but, with Survived & Punished work, it does feel like the work is right in front of us. We do try, but sometimes it is a bit harder to make time for continuing political education beyond our immediate work.

The group has a lot of strengths and weaknesses from where we're all coming. They're really different though, for each individual in the group. We are longtime organizers, newer organizers, academics, direct service workers, policy people, formerly incarcerated and currently incarcerated members, and so on.

MO

Going back to the definitions of accountability that you two offered at the beginning. Are there particular stories that you'd like to share about how you've seen accountability play out in your organizing contexts, positive or negative?

HS

When you're doing defense campaigns or work in relationship with currently and formerly incarcerated people, you think a lot about accountability. How can I be accountable to this person? How can I tell this story in the way that this person wants it to be told? How do I be sensitive to the things they're not ready to talk about or name yet? How do I honestly engage and disagree when I need to, while respecting where that person's coming from? So for example, how do I push back on harmful ideas they have about other people or marginalized groups? When you're in a relationship, an organizing relationship, with someone who is so disempowered by structure, you think a lot about how to be accountable to that person. How to work alongside them in a way that isn't paternalistic or patronizing or condescending, and how to do so in a way that is kind and sensitive and makes that person feel cared about. I think we really value having a high level of accountability to the folks we're supporting, because we know that when we get involved, we are often if not the only then one of the very few lifelines they have to people who still are fighting for them or remembering them.

In terms of accountability between us as members, I think that's something that we're still figuring out together. We've had conversations from the start about the kind of organizing culture we want to have, because a lot of us have been burned before and we want to be able to address conflict upfront. We want to foster an environment where people can air their grievances and get the support they need around it, or at least be able to articulate what they need. And as a feminist abolitionist organization specifically dealing with gender-based violence, how do we deal with violence that may arise within our collective? That has been a longer conversation. In the California chapter, it was a longer process to finalize our internal policies around sexual assault and domestic violence between members.

We are a collective of mostly survivors ourselves. And from what we know of movements, sexual assault and intimate partner violence are happening more often than not. So we can't think of ourselves as too good to fall into that, too. If it happens, how do we deal with it? There were a lot of conversations that felt both very good and easy, and others that were really challenging. But I think we had to hold each other in good faith that we were all doing our best. I feel really good about our process, and where we landed and the conversations, even though it was hard at times. We were doing this all over Zoom during COVID. And part of why we prioritized it was that we didn't feel like we could necessarily bring on board a bunch of new members if we didn't have something like this in place.

Sometimes organizations can grow really quickly, but their organizational development or their structure-building lags a bit behind it. Then something big happens and you don't have anything concrete in place, and it falls apart. As an organization that was founded really because of the way that structures, legal structures, can and are abused to abuse others, we know that all systems can be manipulated, all processes can be manipulated. So how do we create something that is flexible enough and adaptive enough to account for the reality of abuse as well as things like weaponized accountability processes that may actually be getting used as tools of abuse or control themselves? Survivors, like in the criminal legal system, can also be identified as the aggressors in community processes. And in our communities, the language of social justice can be wielded to become another form of exercising power.

MO

That's wonderful. That's so interesting. What did you guys come up with? Is it public, your process?

HS

It's not public, and we have a separate conflict resolution process as well as one specifically for violence and abuse. Because domestic violence and sexual assault are not necessarily regular conflicts. They're not just like, "Me and Emi had a misunderstanding because I said that I was going to work on this and have it done by Friday, but I dropped the ball and didn't communicate, and I've been habitually doing this without really recognizing it." I think that's different in nature from, "This person has been chronically abusing me, verbally tearing me down, battering me in public and in private, or isolating me, threatening me with self-harm or threatening to harm my pets or threatening my job." We wanted to be really sensitive to the dynamics of gender-based, intimate partner violence and sexual violence and the ways that it can really poison an organization from the inside out. It's usually not a single person that tanks an organization or a community. It's really the variety of reactions and nonresponses that surround a situation, in terms of enabling or ignoring or minimizing. I think all of us know someone in the community who has been extremely abusive for a really long time, and everyone knows but no one talks about it. So, some of the things that we talked about and really struggled with were like, what is an adequate consequence that demonstrates we are taking it seriously but does not default to a reactionary expulsion without really knowing more about what has unfolded? Because I think from queer domestic violence, too, you learn pretty quickly that many people have preconceived ideas of who looks like a victim and who doesn't, which are often incorrect. It isn't as easy to recognize as in straight domestic violence. And people use different tactics of control depending on the context, and there are queer-specific, social-justice-specific ones as well. That's something that is really hard to talk about publicly—the weaponization of social justice language.

Some of the questions that we discussed were: If you were sexually assaulted by a member of this group, would you tell anyone? Who would you tell, and would you trust the organization to handle it? And if you would trust the organization to handle it, why, and if you wouldn't trust the organization to handle it, why? So people shared about those things and their prior experiences in different organizations they'd been in. I wanted us to talk about these things with more of a personal sense to it because, because there is a real distancing that happens when you talk about domestic and sexual violence where it's like, "Oh, it happens with people over there. And over here, we are all on the same page. We're all against gender-based violence. We're all against state violence." All that purported unity can provide cover to a lot of different things.

By the end of it, we'd come up with multiple pathways for people to raise concerns or grievances that felt realistic and accomodating of people's actual responses and aren't just limited to filing a formal complaint to one person or one leader. Not everyone is going to be comfortable with one specific channel. So providing as many options and legitimizing as many pathways as possible to raise a concern organizationally was important.

When you're in this group, you have to commit to practicing your values, like in all spheres. You can't just be part of Survived & Punished but be abusive to your partner or sexually assaulting people; that's not in line with our beliefs around feminist practice and gender-based violence. And at what point we ask someone to leave is something we talked about too. I think our process is very flexible and adaptive. But we also have a pretty firm line around having consequences for abuse, and removing people from positions of leadership or public spokesmanship or even membership when needed.

MO

That was great.

EK

I was going to say, Hyejin, what I was thinking as you were talking—first of all, in the last year or so, three different organizations or publications have reached out to me for support coming up with their own accountability policies for addressing violence or abuse, either among their staff or among their authors. So if it's a publication or a press or something like that, what do they do if somebody comes to them and says, "One of your authors assaulted me." And I am curious to know,

Hyejin and Michelle both, if this feels new to you, too. It feels like in the last year, suddenly, people have realized that they need to take some of these steps preemptively, or at least have a policy in place, so that they know how to handle these things as they arise. It's not that those things haven't come up in the past, it's that they probably just ignored them or didn't handle them well. I'm curious to hear from both of you whether you feel like this is something that has more recently become apparent. People are actually starting to take it seriously as something they need to do before violence occurs. I mean, it's imperfect. I'll say also that some of the people who have reached out to me are just doing it to cover their asses. And they're not actually invested in true accountability, or truly changing the conditions of the organizations and our communities, so that violence is less possible or so that accountability is more possible for survivors.

HS

Yeah, I think there has definitely been some heightened energy around it in the past year because of some pretty public deterioration of organizations and processes and all of that. People are more willing to take to social media and speak out than they used to be. But I think these calls for change have been happening for a long, long time. To me, a big part of accountability and this concept of transformative justice is that a huge part of that is actually shifting culture and practice within organizations, within communities. But this collective element where actual structures are challenged or remade together, that gets lost while people get super fixated on how to "rehabilitate" or "heal" or "transform" one individual person who caused harm. I just don't think that putting all your energy into one person is going to translate into the kind of change that I think people are hoping for. Emi and I have talked about this together a lot.

EK

I think you answered, and I would have said similar things. I was just asking because of course, it's been there forever, well beyond my memory, my lifetime even. But I'm noticing it. I'm like—oh, is it because I've been informally supporting survivors for a while, and so people are like, maybe they'll refer me to other people and I'm just hearing about it more? But I actually feel like in the public discourse, I don't know if it's just window dressing or whatever you want to call it, but people are paying some more lip service to it, at least organizationally, on an organizational level, which has just been interesting to note. So I was wondering if you'd seen more of that.

Hyejin, one thing that you and I have spoken about, and that came up for me while listening to you—and this relates back to INCITE! too—is that community accountability, transformative justice, or whatever you want to call it, those concepts are hundreds, thousands of years old—the idea of repairing harm in a community without relying on punishment or exile. But when I think about what we talk about as transformative justice or community accountability now and I trace it back to twenty years ago or a little before that, when I think about it in the context of INCITE!'s work in particular, I think what people kind of forget—and Hyejin, you and I have talked about this—is that a lot of the early conversations about community accountability and non-state-based interventions and community violence or interpersonal violence were mainly formulated by people who were coming out of the domestic violence and sexual assault worlds, who had had that kind of training and background. And so I see some of the issues you're talking about. We've had conversations about it just in terms of getting to a place where they are unable to really identify what abuse is and don't really even understand what that term means. I am not a fan of Sarah Schulman's *Conflict Is Not Abuse* and have even seen that text weaponized in very dangerous ways, including seeing people's abusers literally send copies to others as part of campaigns to discredit their survivors; Aviva Stahl has a good piece in *The New Inquiry* on some of this. Anyhow, truly, conflict is not abuse, just not necessarily in the way Schulman means it. Conflict, abuse, harm, or hurt—all those things are different and call for different responses.

A lot of these concepts are now, twenty-something years later, being taken up by a much wider, larger audience, because they have been popularized via social media or through a different social justice discourse that is not grounded. It's not grounded in that kind of training [around domestic violence and sexual assault], which early INCITE! folks had. And so people take for granted that they know how to center a survivor. They take for granted that they know what abuse is. They take for granted that they know how to support survivors through these processes without causing further harm.

And what they think is the hardest thing to figure out is how to support someone who's caused harm or someone who abuses, or someone who has caused violence, to transform. And so then they are just singularly focused on that. I traced that back to—and this might be totally wrong, but this is my thinking—a lot of ideas and practices growing out of conversations where those things [understandings of domestic violence] were taken for granted, because people at the time did have that very specific training that's needed in order to identify and intervene in abuse dynamics, which are very specific.

I think maybe part of what happened is that, with the disavowal of the white carceral feminist frameworks and practices that needed to happen around the time that INCITE! was formed—and that needed to happen in order to build something new that didn't rely on the criminal legal system or on punishment as a response to violence—with that disavowal or that rejection, we sort of threw the baby out with the bathwater. Meaning that there are some things that are useful from those many decades of thinking and struggle that took place, however problematic or imperfect they were—like the term "abuse."

Abuse means something. It's not just a word that could mean whatever you want it to mean in the moment. There's a reason that it means something, and it just frustrates me to no end that we've gotten to this place where we can't even say that word and have to flatten everything out to "harm"; we've sort of muddied the waters in this way that actually doesn't serve survivors of abuse and rape and violence, or of interpersonal, intimate partner violence, rather. It's gotten away from itself in a way that is actually creating a lot of confusion and increasing violence and harm. One of the things I've encountered personally is a lot of people being afraid to use the term abuse because it's scary, of course, and also being really afraid of mirroring rape-culture thinking and being afraid of false accusations.

Like you said, Hyejin, social justice language does get weaponized in that way a lot of the time, but when that happens, people just sort of wring their hands and act like they don't know what to do and we can't figure it out. But the truth is that if you actually are trained to understand what to look for and how to assess the situation, it's a little bit easier. Like, if abuse means something and it is—like you said—a specific pattern of behavior that is identifiable by people who have the skills and knowledge and training to do that kind of identification, then it helps both the people who are concerned about the false accusations and the people who are surviving violence and abuse, because then we actually have an agreement about what it means. We can actually have a shared understanding of what it means. We know what to look for and we can say, well, that actually isn't abuse. That is this other thing. And we can talk about it and address it in an appropriate way. And when it's abuse, we actually have the skills necessary to address it without causing further harm.

I don't know, those are some things that came up for me. And then I think the other thing you talked about . . . like when I was introduced to community accountability as a term, I understood it to mean that the community enabled or helped, that we all co-created the conditions that allowed harm or abuse or violence to happen. And so therefore, we as a community are all equally responsible for repairing and changing those conditions that allowed that to take place and allowed that to happen in the first place. There's a framework for creating accountable communities, and I feel like that's actually sometimes a little more helpful than talking about transformative justice processes as these sort of stand-alones. Because then it puts the burden mostly on the survivor and the person who caused harm, it individualizes something that is collective, was created collaboratively, and I'm really thinking about how we got from point A to point Z or wherever we are now.

I do think it has a little bit to do with the fact that certain things were taken for granted when some of these practices were first discussed and written down and shared out. It was taken for granted that we understood what abuse is; it was taking for granted that we understand how to support survivors; and it was taken for granted that this was actually a question of a larger collective responsibility to change the conditions that enabled or allowed that to happen in the first place. I don't know. I'm rambling too now, but I am concerned about where we've landed, to be honest, twenty-something years later.

MO

I have lots more questions right now about where we've
landed and what's wrong with it. I'm very interested in
that. You began to speak about it, this sort of confusion and
morass of thinking. And I've seen some of your writing, Emi,
and posts really talking about what Hyejin described as the
weaponization of accountability. Where are we at in thinking
about transformative justice, how did we end up there, and
what's wrong with it? We explored a little bit what's good about
it: A lot more people are talking about sexual harassment,
sexual assault, abuse than were a few years ago. I think you
might have had an impact on that, clearly. You're describing that
process with Survived & Punished that sounds so personal and
so interesting, and exactly the kind of thing every organization
should have done the year it was founded, whenever that
was. So, there are many good things about this moment, very
interesting, very positive things. But then—you referenced
Schulman—there are also a lot of people circulating that have
patterns of harm and use different types of rhetoric in order to
cover themselves or protect themselves.

HS

To me, the language of transformative justice, the language
of social justice, these ideological frameworks we have—they
are all tools for power. It's not just how we think about power,
it's also the way that thinking about power actually structures
relationships of power themselves. These ideas, whether they're
around gender justice, or transformative justice, or racial
justice, or prison abolition—all these things came from the need
to identify and articulate power as it is now, and also to make an
intervention into it.

So I think what's happening here is a power struggle over
the terrain of what transformative justice is and what abuse
even is, actually. It's not being articulated that way, but there
are various camps around it that disagree or have alignment in
numerous ways. What we're seeing is a power struggle over
it where certain people are like, call-outs are all bad, they're
carceral, asking someone to step down or de-platform is the
same thing as sending them to prison. And then other people who
are like, call-outs are all inherently good, cancel culture does not
exist, and call-out culture is an avenue for the most silenced and

the most disenfranchised to really speak out, and it's their one way of trying to level the playing field. There are grains of truth to each kind of framework in how teaching and accountability are talked about. There are grains of truth, which is why it's so hard to disentangle for people what actually makes sense.

As a broader web of communities that are largely queer, trans people of color, leftists of various stripes, we are problem-solvers in various ways. We want to solve so many things. And as organizers, that's what you're trained to do. An organizer is trying to shift the relations of power to alleviate suffering, to address social harms, to change the balance of power. And what that can translate to within these more interpersonal issues, that aren't about a big outside enemy like a bank or a president, is that that urge to problem solve can lead to skipping a bunch of steps out of urgency, when you actually need to slow down and sit with what happened. Like Emi was speaking to, this dovetails with a general avoidance of discomfort, fear of losing community, fear of failure or looking bad. With abolition and transformative justice gaining more visibility and popularity, it means there are more people entering at disparate points in the conversation, with less of us having the same starting point or foundation.

EK

I agree with everything Hyejin said. Again, Hyejin and I have been in conversation about some of this for a while. I learned a lot through those conversations. I guess I can speak to my own personal experience; I think it kind of reflects where the conversation is in some ways, or where some of the conversations I'm observing are. I wanted to share a point that I realized in the last couple of years, that my way of relating to this idea of transformative justice, even abolition and community accountability, was actually pretty theoretical for a long time. For many, many years, when I was very young coming up through INCITE!, they were ideas and practices that I supported. I definitely supported different accountability processes and TJ-style interventions throughout the years, but I never fully understood them until I attempted one of my own. It completely changed the way I relate to these concepts. We're all coming from our lived experience. That's actually what taught me the most about this, and that's what shifted my thinking in the most profound ways.

For a long time, I did buy into these ideas that I currently find really problematic and that are kind of dominating some of the conversations—that we just have to look at the root causes of someone's trauma and then we'll get to this happy place where everyone's trauma is healed and harm no longer occurs. To me, this mirrors the way you think when you are trapped in a cycle of abuse. For example, when you're in an abusive relationship, you keep asking them to change, you hope for them to change. They don't. You keep trying and then they do something to make you think that they'll change, like agreeing to go to therapy for a bit. And then you try again and you try again. And then years pass and you're still in the same dynamic. The goalposts move and nothing really changes. So then you get out, and someone says, "Well, if we just do this process, they will finally change." It's very alluring because it mirrors the logic that's kept you in the relationship or abusive dynamic. It's comfortable, and comforting to think that this intervention might be the thing that finally interrupts the harm. We live in a solutions-oriented culture, and this can feel like an easy way out of a problem far more complex than many of us are willing to admit or grapple with. There are people doing that grappling, but I think some of that complexity can get buried in ways that can have serious consequences.

I've heard people talk about accountability and violence and say things like,"The first thing you do when harm occurs is you look at the root cause of the harm," which I think is a bit misguided. Actually, the first thing you do when harm occurs is you stop the harm. You make sure the person who is harmed is centered and safe and OK. And then maybe you turn to the person who caused the harm or the person who used violence, and the person who abused or raped or assaulted somebody or harassed somebody. You turn your attention to them and then you see, OK, what can we do to make sure this doesn't happen again. We're skipping important steps.

I think that carries over into conversations about abolition, too. One of the things Hyejin has talked about, and we've had conversations about, is the fact that people talk about abolition, but not everyone's talking to or centering the voices of people inside, people who have survived incarceration. What we're seeing are the growing pains of people I think actually coming face-to-face with what that looks like in real time and in really practical ways through people's experiences. So, I don't really know where we are, except that I think I agree with what Hyejin said, it's a period of reckoning for a lot of people. And I'll speak from my own experience, again: The last few years in particular have been a period of reckoning for me with what I inherited and what I internalized and understood about myself and about abolition and violence and abuse, and how we address those things in our communities, and then sort of unlearning some of those things, and having to look at how those concepts do or do not translate into practice in my own life. And how different it is when you're the survivor in an attempted accountability process, really just asking for the cycle of harm to be interrupted, and then having everyone tell you that you're asking for punishment, realizing that we haven't done some of the work that's necessary to create conditions that will make it safe for many survivors to undertake a process like that without being further harmed or traumatized. So I don't know. I don't know where we're at.

I feel like we're muddling our way through all of the increased visibility, and the ways I've seen people adopt this language without having the lived experience and the practice to inform how that language is used. I feel like we're at a place where it's in flux, but I appreciate Hyejin's framing of it as necessary and natural. I don't think I'm hopeful, but I do think that just hearing you talk has made me sort of rethink my despair, the despair I've been feeling about it over the last couple of years.

MO

Thank you both so much for this time and the tremendous amount of wisdom and insight to this conversation. And honestly, it's been extremely worthwhile.

Kim
Diehl

Kim Diehl is a queer Black feminist in her
forties who has organized primarily in the South
for more than twenty years, both in the labor
movement and as a member of a Maoist organization.
She describes her entry into abolition and
transformative justice as coming out of her union
work. She is on the national board of Critical
Resistance and is currently enrolled in a seminary
in New York.

KIM DIEHL

The abolitionist community when I came along, when I started
twenty years ago, was like, I don't know, a very, very small
number of people forming the basis for what is now lines of
thought around transformative justice and accountability and
shutting down the prison-industrial complex. It's a spiderweb,
I would say, sort of blossoming or getting formed in a
more structured way, like twenty years ago, where there
was actually funding and multiple layers of movement
involvement. It wasn't only academics talking about it . . .
it was influenced by formerly incarcerated folks, people
who had been doing a lot of Black nationalist work, the
Malcolm X Grassroots Movement, you know, already so
many different convergences.

MAX FOX

Totally. Yeah, around the millennium, right?

KD

Yeah, in 1988 there was the first conference looking at ending
the prison-industrial complex.

MF

1998?

KD

Yeah, that was the one that was called Critical Resistance and
the organization was born out of that. And then, in 2000 or
so, I was doing some investigative journalism for community
organizing and labor organizing, looking at the new rights of
prison labor, convict labor, private prisons, how they are really
coming out of the South. You know, the corporations were in
Tennessee . . . and anyway, that got me connected with the folks
who formed Critical Resistance and problems in there. So that
was kind of how I got connected.

MF

Yeah. Not that we have to go directly in order, but that leads us
right into the first question, if you don't mind. How did you get
there? What's your personal background that brought you to
that, to where you were in 1998?

Yeah, so I was at the University of North Carolina at Chapel Hill in '95, a junior, and there were housekeepers and groundskeepers that were organizing a union. As a student, I helped do student solidarity work. And the issues that the housekeepers were fighting for were, you know, much better pay, better working conditions. They did not want to be contracted out. They didn't want to be privatized. So that was the fight. And I was like, what is this privatized thing? That really got me connected with some organizers in the South, some more veteran organizers who were concerned about that and did some community research, you know, to plant some seeds around what was happening. Out of that, I was then working at the Institute for Southern Studies, which was the organization that had the magazine called *Southern Exposure*. It's still around—I haven't seen it in print anymore but it exists online as facingsouth.org. It's a leftist magazine with progressive coverage of issues in the South that folks are also organizing on. So, you know, our interest in privatization wasn't necessarily because, oh, people should care about workers. We're saying we don't want our public services privatized. And it was mostly Black workers, and this was all in the South. So that can be connected with Black radicals who had been involved in the New Communist Movement and were helping to provide support and organize support for the housekeepers and groundskeepers and in conjunction with UE, the union, United Electrical Workers, they formed Local 150. And I was just part of that. It just happened to be a time when I was in the right place at the right time. I was interested in labor issues because my mom was a public school teacher. And so all this happened in North Carolina in the late '90s, early 2000s, and was really influenced—deliberately influenced—by Black communists who were trying to organize the South. It was a model of organizing where they were not in the front, it was the workers out in the front, they were doing the leadership development. I got to learn how to sit with them and be in the conversation to be in the planning. And that was how I got radicalized. It was with the Black Workers for Justice.

That's amazing.

KD

They're still around. Yeah, it is amazing. It's like, who gets to
live that, you know? It's just amazing to have these relationships
with people who deliberately decided to leave their homes in
the North, some more in the North or somewhere in like West
Virginia or wherever—but they had an organized decision:
We're going to go organize the South. We're going to go live
our lives and struggle in the Deep South, and we're going to
work as rank-and-file workers. We're going to be working at
the post office, in the auto works. We're going to do all of this as
working-class Black people. And so that was where I started to
create my own political outlook, which I guess I would describe
as queer-Black-feminist Black nationalism. I very much learned
about what the concept of a nation is. You know, what is the
definition of a nation, how that applied to Black people. And
really, you know, just understood how I saw my world in a
much different way because I grew up in the South. Yeah, from
Florida, I saw . . . I just was able to put a framework around the
Southern apartheid.

MF

Totally.

KD

Anyway, so the early 2000s is when some of these private
companies, like the Hospital Corporation of America (HCA),
actually had the same model for privatizing public hospitals
that they had to privatize prisons. They call them Corrections
Corporation of America (CCA). So there's HCA, CCA.
They fucking came out of Nashville. Same exact people,
same players, and they basically created the blueprint for
privatization of public services. Wackenhut for private security,
Maximus for social services, Lockheed Martin . . . They
were starting to really look at other ways to make money, the
federal government, so they started privatizing child support
enforcement and they were horrible, horrible, horrible,
horrible employers. Lockheed Martin fucking doing child
support enforcement.

MF

Wow.

KD

Yeah. So I got my hands deep into the privatization of public services for a good while, and then I also became a member of Freedom Road, which is how I met Michelle. It was the folks out of Black Workers for Justice. That was a formation that Freedom Road and folks from the New Communist Movement had created. And I also did some queer organizing in the South, but I did that just for a little while. It was not something that I felt really spoke to me as far as a job, to be a professional queer. I don't know if you know Southerners On New Ground (SONG)?

MF

Oh, sure.

KD

Yeah. So I was the codirector for them in my mid-twenties. I didn't have that experience, but it was cool. I love the South. I got to go around and develop my deep, deep, deep love for Southern queer folks of color and all the ways that we resist and the beautiful things that folks are part of. But my favorite place to go is to go visit the South. I live in Brooklyn right now and I'm happy to be in Brooklyn, but my heart is in those twelve states of the former Confederacy, and particularly Miami.

MF

Miami—is that where you were in Florida, where you grew up?

KD

Yes. So [for] my childhood, I was in Miami. My family moved to Central Florida for about eight years. And that was horrible. It was when the rise of the Christian Right was happening and I was questioning and it was just a horrible place for one, and my dad was really involved in the church, very conservative. But I left and went all the way to South Carolina, to the College of Charleston, and then I transferred to UNC. That was the furthest North I ever lived until I moved here six years ago.

After I worked at SONG, I ended up going to work for a union because of a friend. I was looking for work and she was like, I am working for Service Employees International Union (SEIU), and there's a campaign here, and we need a communications person. I didn't know what communications really meant. I mean, I was like, I work for a magazine. But I didn't know. I had been involved in organizing, but I didn't know beyond how to make a flyer. And especially with a monster union like SEIU. But I did have a very, very rigorous training; it was hard and my ego was bruised often, but I did learn the craft of communications and I got to actually go to California for a janitor strike in like 2006 or 2007. Their contract was up. They went on strike. It was the really radical janitors with black and white strike flags. I'd never seen militancy like that, ever. It was a week filled with rolling strikes throughout Silicon Valley in the Bay. And every day was like thousands of janitors walking off the job, stopping, stopping the scabs from coming in to work at night. They were doing night shifts, so we would hang out there at night in Silicon Valley. It was cold at this office park for Google, and we'd just go and sit. And these workers stopped the trucks, literally stopped these SUVs with the scabs. They started taking the air out of the tires and just surrounding them. And the cops were right there. The union president, Mike Garcia, he passed away, rest in power. And this was just like how we strike here in California. It was fucking beautiful.

MF

Damn. Wow, yeah, that's an intense picket line to hold.

KD

And then, what was fun, was just how the workers had such a great sense of humor around the chants . . . We would like to say a name like, "Max, escucha, estamos en la lucha." We were on Stanford's campus, so they started making up names. They're like, "Christina, Stephanie, Jenny, escucha." They started calling out all of these white people, like, "Chad, escucha . . . " Oh my God, I loved it. It was so much fun. And they won. They won the contract. Yeah. Then in Miami I also worked for a union and there was a janitors' strike that was never . . . I don't know if you knew about that, but in 2007 or 2008, there was a hunger strike. They actually went on hunger strike. University of Miami.

I might have heard about that. That was pretty national kind
of . . .

Just to get recognized, right? To form a fucking union. They
went on hunger strike. So, like, a lot of my experiences have
been around labor organizing and then with Critical Resistance,
the organization that I helped form in like 2000, I was just
like . . . actually I mean, we don't have to write this, but I had
mad crushes on people, you know . . .

That's classic.

I mean, like, everywhere I turn.

That's how it goes.

Beautiful, fucking brilliant people. I was like, "You want me
to come to a meeting? OK, yes. I will get my flirt on." But
mostly I just sucked in all of the knowledge and training of our
movement, and I mean, that's what it is all about. Having this
big old crush on like Ruthie Gilmore, you know. I could just sit
side by side with Ruthie Gilmore and be like, whatever Ruthie
says I'm down with, you know. Rose Braz, she's passed on, big
ol' crush on Rose. But, you know, they took me seriously and
I took them seriously. And we had a very fun time, really good
stories, because, you know, in California, there's interesting
characters that show up to events. So we have one in Fresno
and there's some group of folks who might have been Rainbow
[Family], they might have been Rainbow children. The Rainbow
people are a little bit deadhead-y, but like, further out there.
They're real happy, the Rainbow people. But they are involved,
they'll turn out for you. We don't really know where they
will. They're very decentralized. They don't exactly have,
like, formalized politics, right? They're not Marxist-Leninist.
Anyways, yeah, they came and they were really high, like really

tripping. And it was a conference to look at the priorities of building prisons in people of color communities. So Fresno, lots of farmworkers, farmworker organizations coming and abolitionists and the Rainbow people came and one of them took the microphone at lunch and she just was like, "I have a sandwich. I have a sandwich . . ." over and over again, and then Ruthie got the microphone from her. But yeah, that was just being in spaces where there was this real intersectionality that was built out of relationships. Rose, who was one of the founders of Critical Resistance, was going to Fresno and organizing and really talking to the people and building relationships and saying, "I know y'all are really concerned about the pesticides and what's happening in their communities, did you know that there's also the prison that wants to buy land here and imagine what that . . ." You know? And the same thing when you organize Critical Resistance conferences. We had one in the South and went door-knocking in Tremé, and I just followed the lead of folks, and you know, just did what folks asked of me, and if it was to make peanut butter jelly sandwiches, cool, if it was to flyer, great, if it was to take the microphone away . . . That's how I basically was formed as an abolitionist, being around those folks. I don't really have much campaign experience as far as stopping a prison or the gang injunctions that have happened here in New York; I haven't really done much chapter-based organizing, which is how Critical Resistance was organized. I've done all of my work as a national member through different committees that are very behind the scenes, helping to create the structure, a relatively nonhierarchical structure as much as possible . . .

MF

For these chapters?

KD

For the staff, I'd organize them. Some chapters had organizers, paid organizers. So it would be like, what's the relationship between the national staff and, of course, the people who are in the local chapters? And how do we build accountability? There weren't any easy answers and there were some really hard decisions and hard struggles, and then even within the staff . . . But that's where I would say a lot of the work I've done around accountability and developing principles around internal accountability and how to have processes for resolving disputes has really been done. I've done it enough to know that I don't know shit [*laughs*]. I have so much mad respect for real conflict resolution facilitators. You know, I can facilitate, but I don't have anywhere near the skills to do a hardcore facilitation if there has been physical, interpersonal harm. There are principles, but shit goes down around like theft or personal violation and harm like that. That's from Mariame Kaba. I think—also because, you know, I realize my place in the movement around abolition too is like, I'm a family member of somebody inside, my brother did time a couple of times, but I haven't myself ever faced the type of harm where, if we're talking about sexual assault, physical violence, things like that, war, I can really be as . . . The role I have is to be a co-conspirator. And how do I hold that space and listen to the folks who have worked through being violated and harmed? How they would want justice, but in the parameters of . . . ? How do we not rely on policing, punishment, and shame to be how we respond? Because justice has to be something other than that. It's the only way we can survive as humans.

Reading the questions you have here, and a lot of them really speak to very present-day questions, and there are ones that I think are hard to answer over email. For example, I've had exchanges with comrades about abolition and they're like, "Well, my daughter was assaulted and mugged and we can't move the masses by saying 'defund the police.' We have to be able to have police, because my daughter was assaulted." And that's not something that I want to be like, "OK," and have an exchange over email about. And in a lot of ways, he's right; where we're at is not in a place where any of us have the skills yet to imagine something else, and I don't necessarily think treading on his pain is helpful. To say, "No, you're wrong." But I do want to have those conversations in especially red circles, where folks are not as familiar with abolition at all or policing—especially with labor, that's huge. How do you reconcile the fact that American Federation of State, County and Municipal Employees (AFSCME), the union, has its finger on the pulse of cops? Yeah. And they are at the helm of creating some of the worst lynching laws. Like a *lynching*. Yeah. So that's the accountability I want to wrestle with. Especially in the South, where Black folks are at the head of so many schools and principals and are hardcore about cap- . . . what is that when they allow . . . ?

MF

Corporal punishment.

KD

Corporal punishment. Yeah. I mean it's like, those are Black people. You know, that's like Black-led school districts in Louisiana, Arkansas, Mississippi.

MF

That's a good point. Yeah.

KD

Yeah. So not sure where I was going with that, but that's what I want to be looking at.

MF

Yeah, and that's fascinating. I mean, so you got there basically from talking about Critical Resistance.

KD

Yeah.

MF

You said so much that was really fascinating there. And I don't want to lose track of any of it, but you said that basically you learned abolition from your participation there, right? So that wasn't necessarily a component of the political education you'd received prior?

KD

No, it wasn't. No, absolutely not. It was in conjunction. It was an interesting merging; some overlap might have been because Malcolm X Grassroots Movement (MXGM) was doing a lot around CopWatch and things like that.

MF

And you had a relationship with them?

KD

Yeah I mean, as a Black-led . . . they were probably the biggest Black radical org [of that period], so they really led our leaders on questioning the police in a different way than Black revolutionaries from a trade union background have, which is where my political education really came from. I would say the bridge would be the writings and publications and influence MXGM had on me, and then also Critical Resistance—I would say that is how those things kind of happen. And, you know, a lot of it was sort of parallel at the same time. But I'm looking back and they just didn't merge, you know? It still is different circles, like Black trade-unionist threads are definitely not in circles looking at violence and alternatives to punishment.

MF

Yeah. Why do you think that is? That's interesting.

KD

I mean, part of it speaks to . . . I think the movement around abolition was either academic bourgeoisie and the lumpenproletariat—so people who were, you know, really on the margins, not able to work, underground—and Black trade unionists, working-class, folks with jobs organizing in their shops and the public sector.

MF

Yeah, but then they had . . . I mean, presumably they might have heard about Critical Resistance stuff you were putting on and maybe there was interest. But you're saying there's no merger ultimately. It's fascinating.

KD

I know, I know. I think, too, that a lot of the people who were doing work around violence against women were women and trade unionists were men. And these were, you know, women looking at healing justice as an intersection, and how do we define a society that provides resources to people so that we don't have to steal and we have what we need in order to have mental health resources and schools, housing, food. And on the other side, it was like, fighting for schools, housing, food. It was very much around patriarchy. Even though there

were folks that were formerly incarcerated, that was a lot of
dudes leading that along with a lot of women, so there was a
struggle for sure. But this is a different . . . folks that come
out of prison, formerly incarcerated, don't have a whole lot
of structural power. Cultural power, yes. But trade unionists
dudes, they come with big boots.

I could go on about unions, it's really sad, you know. It's a
moment of severe, severe problems. Maybe we could even call
it famine. I don't know. Would this be a famine for the union
membership? It's something . . .

MF

Yeah, it's not good. That is really fascinating. I want to see if I
can get some insight about . . . You said one of the things you
did with Critical Resistance was help set up these accountability
processes and structures. But you were learning from the other
people there about specifically abolitionist or TJ principles as
you're developing them, right?

KD

All of that. Yeah.

MF

I guess I'm curious, in your mind at the time, were you like,
"Oh, I can apply this prior model, here's some formal thing
that'll work." Was it just total experimentation, or how did . . .

KD

You know, it was more like I took the lead from folks who
knew. Then we tested it. So it was more of the implementation,
putting it into a committee, seeing how it worked. Test, go back,
test, go back, and reflect and refine. And over twenty years, it's
evolved. There is a living document that's on [the website for]
Critical Resistance, accountability and harm principles, that
folks applying for the job but also being oriented to the job have
as principles. So it was not a one-time thing, it was an iterative
process. Also, at the same time, what was happening when
Critical Resistance was formed was that, just a few years later,
INCITE! Women of Color Against Violence, was also formed.
That formation really helped us as far as developing our line and
thinking around accountability and harm internally. So it was

a convergence of several different things. But yeah, INCITE! was a huge influence, because folks in Critical Resistance were involved with INCITE!, back and forth, you know. And that's how I know of Mariame Kaba and her work with that whole sphere. Like I said, with the spiderweb, I was in the part of the web where I was taking that and trying to bureaucratize it in a way to structure and systematize.

MF

It's interesting, would you say that was sort of your trade union formation coming to be useful?

KD

Definitely. I love systems and structures; also, doing communications for a living, there have to be areas of work in the production schedule so that we all kind of have a trajectory we're going toward. It's like a daisy chain, all these little soft points. That's how I think I've had to lend a hand to this work, trying to systematize it somewhat, but using the series that I was taught. A lot of Mao, a lot of Mao. Mao is a great thinker as far as systematizing and how to test, take from the masses, test. Unity, struggle, unity. Lots of that [*laughs*].

MF

I love that. Can you say a little bit more about where the Mao is in these systems you set up? What's an example, maybe?

KD

There's a couple. I'm just trying to piece together my memories . . . They're in fragments. Well, here's the big one. When Critical Resistance was being formed, everyone wanted to be a chapter and there was this incredible burst of energy. It was a very charismatic moment everywhere, from Australia to Scotland, all throughout the South especially; there were formations of people who wanted to form a chapter. And we needed to figure out what the criteria of a chapter was. The main premise was that it had to be centered on folks who were directly impacted: people had to be formerly incarcerated or have family members who were. And then, the other was that the work couldn't help to prop up the prison-industrial complex, because there were some groups that were like, "We're lefty priests and clergy who don't believe in prisons, but we have prison ministries. Can we bring Critical Resistance for the ministries?" And it was like, how to look at contradiction, you know, Mao. Like, there probably would be too much of a bourgeois influence to have priests come into a prison, or religious people come into a prison, and be talking about abolition. The abolition had to come from the people or in partnership with the people who were directly impacted. So, yeah, that was one.

It wasn't easy because we were pretty liberal about who could be in a chapter and there were some messy places. And that was where we had to put into action accountability and how do you measure accountability to the people, you know? You don't get to have a block party that has Critical Resistance logos everywhere, but call the cops to protect the block party, you know? And we had to do that around conferences. We would do trainings at conferences around: How do we keep ourselves safe? How do we actually put it into action, or what are the protocols? How do you call in people if you've been harmed? Who are the people that protect us? And we did actually have some Black nationalist groups at times come and do . . . because they were trained, they were former Black Panthers, they knew self-defense. So we would have those types of resources from the people to help teach us about self-defense and to be the people who did that self-defense. That was a huge learning for me. Normally for organizing, we have to have permits and have the police do the escorting. And in this case, it really is not part of our principles.

What else? Internally, having staff conflict, folks who just don't show up or are untimely, you know, it's about building processes where folks can feel heard but then at the same time might be able to say: That's bullshit. And I feel like when there aren't processes there, it's like we get to pretend that what we're witnessing isn't happening, especially if it is somebody who was formerly incarcerated [or] hasn't had real, traditional work, necessarily. And be able to give the space to let folks do what they need to do, and be free and be flexible, but then at the same time, we're also accountable to this chapter and what the chapter's wanting and having those really hard conversations, a number of times. It's exhausting. So I get why in corporate culture you have "One strike, you're out." That shit is so tiring. It's not easy work, you know. But it's just.

And those experiences ended up somehow crystallized in the
formal procedures you used in the documents.

KD

Yeah. I mean, yes, and there was fallout, you know, because
folks are good organizers [*laughs*]: they organize the community,
and there's lots of community demand to keep this person, for
example, or people. It's been twenty years, so there's plenty of
people. I mean, in one chapter, there was literally someone stealing.
And the chapter members were like, "OK." It's like, no. But the
preface we have is we need to get this person help and support. And
there was an intervention, rather than firing them. There was an
intervention. I think they ended up going to rehab because it was
drug-related and they couldn't be a part of the organization for five
years. And she's come back and it's really good to see her. But we
took space, you know, and she's active now. It was at a time when
the chapter was actually really involved in going up against the
police department, one of the most well-funded police departments
in the nation. And there were break-ins happening and there was
surveillance and mysterious things happening to the office. And so
to have somebody also using . . . we had to put our principles first
and really have an intervention. But it wasn't about like, "OK, we're
going to file charges against you." You know what I mean? That
area hasn't had a real functioning chapter since that happened, and
that was like eight years ago.

MF

Because of this intervention?

KD

Well, because of a multitude of things. But after that
intervention, the doors closed. And then there was a series of
mediated conversations and there wasn't a full resolution, but
there was mending. In accountability procedures, you can't
necessarily guarantee that there will be a tidy ending at all,
but is there mending? Not for healing, but is there mending?
And can we at least part ways for a little while? And then
the same with the staff person I was talking about before,
who was just not showing up and it didn't work. There was a
whole community of folks in that city that really loved this

dude because he had done amazing work in his lifetime with
the people in his community, you know, in that city, he'd
really done transformative work, especially around young
folks not being involved in gangs and really organizing them
to get politicized—some fucking badass shit. And yet in this
particular role, it was obvious that this wasn't his jam. But he
organized a lot of people and we don't have a chapter there
either, so it's like, there are good happy endings. But there is a
principle, you know.

MF

So at some point, there comes this choice, where you have to . . .

KD

Yeah, the common good over the personality. And the
organization's still here ten years, twenty years later; an
abolitionist organization is still here and thriving and has
helped create a movement around abolition. I don't necessarily
think that when people say they're abolitionists, they really
are. That's a process, and it's like, you can't be an abolitionist
but then be really happy that the cop that killed George Floyd
is going to prison. That's not abolition. It's not. What we're
after is a different type of justice, but it's still a dream to see
a conversation happening in the United States. A mass-scale
looking at the role of the police. Because I didn't think in my
lifetime we would be questioning, "What does it take for us to
be safe?" That was the question that we all seeded with: What's
good for these instances? (What do you think you need to be
safe?) And like, that shit is actually . . . that question is actually
happening. And in some ways, it's almost because the police are
killing us. It's like, Ida B. Wells wasn't having to ask people if the
police keep us safe because there was like a clear understanding.
So I'm not saying this is going to lead to our liberation, because
in so many ways we've been so fucking brainwashed to think
that police are keeping us safe when in reality Paul Robeson, Ida
B. Wells, they all knew that their job was to protect property and
white people, you know.

MF

And it is. Yeah, I mean, that's real. I'm sorry, it's very heavy,
but what were you saying also . . . I mean, last summer, it

appeared kind of miraculous that everybody was—like you're saying, not everybody who says they're an abolitionist is—but somehow word got out that that's a thing you could be, you know? It's wild.

KD

It's wild.

MF

I guess my question is, you've been in this for a very long time. You've helped so much with the shaping of it. What are some things that happened with Critical Resistance and the specific attempts at doing accountability or transformative justice that people are going to be encountering themselves as they all start on their new abolitionist journey? Or, what's a relevant lesson that comes from the experience you have?

KD

I think it's really about collectively deconditioning ourselves around the carceral state and all the ways we are shaped by it. That's an ongoing process. It's something that I have to undo every day because, for example, I like true crime. You know? It's my guilty pleasure. And I also understand that its role is to glorify the police and to keep people thinking that there are inherently bad, mentally ill people who can't control themselves and that they have to be caged. And I consume that media knowing full well what its purpose is, but in community, I can also see how others are upset with it, and check in with it and ask how I can dismantle it, right? Like, I know that this is a whole form of entertainment that many of us consume; I can really relate to people on that level where we get to check each other. So there's just a collective knowing that we have to do this all the time, and we have to make compromises. And being able to make principled compromises to call the police or to report something, you know, it's got to be a real communal decision around how we handle the police and policing. It's not up to me, you know what I'm saying? I don't know if I'm explaining myself right, but the folks who are directly harmed need to be involved in passing through their stages of anger and grief and rage at being held, and also having a process to be able to see the fullness of what accountability can be. So that, if I were talking to someone who was just getting involved with abolition, it's like: Where do you feel resentment and what do you want to do with your resentment? Are you fueled by anger and emotions? Because abolition is not about "I'm pissed off and I want to see justice these ways." It's a politics. And we don't give a fuck about what you feel. It's about a long-term rebuilding of society that isn't about individual emotion, but about really looking at and imagining ways that we could start to identify the behaviors in folks early and figure out how to manage them or all of the things, the factors, that go into what makes somebody decide they want to rape someone or be a serial rapist. None of that is ever researched. None of that is ever talked about. None of that is a real, actual science, you know? And then as far as all the rest of what we call "crime," it's economic factors. So how do we actually look at that? What are the factors that went into this person actually going into stealing those shoes or that car or that truck? Because pretty much 99 percent of the time it's about capitalism. People feel like they either deserve it and they're going to get it because they deserve it, or they really need it because they're hungry and they need a place to live and will do whatever it takes to survive. Those are the big picture questions. It's not about emotions.

MF

OK, yeah, thank you. This is kind of related to that, but you've mentioned in some of these stories you're telling me about these interventions that you did and your whole introduction to the process . . . We've been interested in this question of failure and how accountability processes always somehow seem to, like you said . . . it's always a messy ending, at best. Sometimes people think that that discredits the attempt, and sometimes people think it doesn't really change how you get to understand what's going on. But how do you think about failure in this context? What do you think it means or what does it show?

KD

I think it's easy to say we failed if it's not grounded in what it is long-term we're trying to build. Everything's a failure if we think about it hard enough. It's our role as folks who are not capitalist and following a design of rugged individualism to always put it back to the common good and measure our decisions against that and really figure out: Is the common good being defined by someone who is, in this moment, very hurt or harmed and we're trying to make them feel better? Or is the common good about this long-term thing that we really believe we're building? And it's not any easier; I'd say it's very difficult. What I want to figure out in movement spaces is how we build those skills—have a facilitation skill, a communication skill . . . How can we be able to talk about, like, I'm really pissed off, but maybe in a week I'm not going to be as pissed off. So can we have this meeting later. Or, how do we stop ourselves from retaliating to feel better? Even though every single thing we see is all about self-gratification and we feel we are entitled to having our say no matter what. Because I need to have my say and I can go on Facebook and have my say, because I have this fucking account, but I think that we don't have to have our say and we can still maintain dignity, we can still be whole, complete human beings, and if we were wrong, it doesn't mean that we have to be right. That is not justice—making sure that Max, you got to say "That's really a great retort" to someone. And you were right. But that's not fucking justice. That's not liberation. And it's the people who have been systemically wronged who have to have their voices heard, you know?

That's what I feel is so, so sad right now. And I see it in movement spaces, because we're going to hurt each other. Like, oh, my god, we just lived through Trump who's like the worst public figure in the history of public figures, maybe. I want to say he is. And we had to be bombarded with this shit all the time. Of course, every now and then, I'm going to feel like I want to write a mean tweet, right? In the grand scheme of things, what's that gonna do? I feel like that's the socialist or communist discipline, asking, How is this in the long run for the common good? And it does require a very disciplined way of holding ourselves in a space. I don't think in the United States we have much experience doing that at all. Holding ourselves in a space and being able to move in a space where we're not just a bunch of single organisms. This country's fucked up, it's really sick, you know, the hyper-individualism . . . When I think of some of the shit I've

seen ... And then on top of that, the white supremacy. Lord,
yeah, Christianity ... And I'm in seminary, Max! Yeah, that's
all I would say for folks: How do we hold ourselves in a space
that's really about the common good and community, and
how do we have the self-awareness and then the willingness
to fail and be vulnerable and to be like, Max, I feel like I was
a real asshole at the meeting, did I come off too snippy? How
do you handle these situations? This ongoing conversation
is a really important part of abolitionism. Like, I'm just a
worker among workers. Yeah, I have some unique shit, I'm a
badass. I'm also a very flawed human being. I don't see a lot of
things. So that's what I love about having my experience with
Critical Resistance. I got to see some things that I never would
have seen from my upbringing, you know, being twenty
something, my upbringing in central Florida. Abolitionism is
a whole new world.

MF

See new things in terms of holding yourself in a space, or ... ?

KD

Oh, seeing new things like how community decisions are
made, like how we have several days together where we have
built-in mechanisms so there's full participation of folks who
are cast aside, you know, folks who have been really brutalized
by capitalism in the United States. I mean, I feel like there is
a whole unseen world, the prison system that a lot of us don't
ever interact with. And for folks coming out of it into this world
and then trying to find a political home, it's extremely difficult.
Especially with folks who are civilians who don't have a record.
So what I've seen with my work at Critical Resistance is a real
centering of people who have both feet inside and outside,
you know, who are on probation and not far from being on
probation. It's got people inside, always. It's a precarious
life. And it's very cruel. Folks bring that back with them. So
how do we build? I've seen folks learn how to really express
themselves in front of a group and be able to talk about what's
going on in their communities. And do it in a way where they
really show how much they love their community and it's not
people talking about them, which is what I think the majority
of what we deal with looks like.

MF

Sure. Yeah.

KD

So that's what I mean. Like growing up a middle-class biracial kid in central Florida, a college education, and yeah, my brother was inside, but I never felt like I was necessarily close to doing time. So, I'm learning how to be be in a space where I step back, I'm not the expert.

MF

But like you're saying, you still need to be a co-conspirator at some level, you still need to be able to be part of that community that is holding these conversations.

KD

Yeah, definitely. Definitely.

MF

Yeah. I mean, that's really ... If you can get there, that's such a powerful thing. I think that's the thing that people struggle with how to carry out, but that's wonderful that that was the sort of gift that's here ...

KD

And keep giving. In some ways we're doing it well, in some ways not so much. You know, it's mixed. Some chapters have folks who were formerly incarcerated and there's some that are like ... not really.

MF

That's what you mean by not doing that well?

KD

Yeah, as far as maintaining relationships, memberships. It's mixed. But what a privilege to be around to keep trying to do it better each time and to have ... Emotions get raw in organizing spaces because so much is on the line. And I've always felt like at Critical Resistance there were people who knew how to handle really tough stuff, and later I was able to handle really tough stuff, and if we didn't know, we knew where to turn.

I just feel like that's a beautiful, soft pillow to land on with transformative justice. You know, we have certainly stubbed our toe here, wow, we fell flat on our face. But we kind of know what to do. I think that's part of how we've been able to stay around this long. On the accountability level.

MF

And that's the accountability, you mean?

KD

Yeah, to be able to have folks . . . Right now, I know that there are struggles on staff. This is an ongoing thing, where there's someone on staff who feels like they aren't being seen, their expertise isn't being seen, for example, and they're struggling with meeting chapter goals or having members come—just like any kind of organizer struggle. "Right now, people aren't calling me back, dammit, I'm just mad. And I have to check in with somebody about that. And I hate that I have to check in with somebody about that." And the resentment gets created based on the stories we tell ourselves when things aren't necessarily going our way—that we're right, and we start othering, we start really believing that the situation is much bigger and broader than what it really is. And that it's a political situation, you know? But this is not indigenous to Critical Resistance. This is a lot of us as young organizers being like, I know how to organize this chapter. I don't need to check in. I don't need a supervisor or mentor or check-in person. And so we play with it. Volunteers check in with stuff. I've made the rounds with someone who has weekly check-ins with a staff person as a volunteer, so it kind of depersonalizes the dynamic. And the new person kind of airs out their grievances so that I can actually help coach them into a place of honesty.

MF

Unity, struggle, unity.

KD

Yeah.

Not to push too hard on it, but do you find that these Maoist things are still useful to you and the daily work of this stuff?

KD

Always. I am always calculating the balance of forces in all kinds of realms of making decisions based on those, or at least helping groups make decisions based on the balance of forces, and definitely exploring contradiction. There was a contradiction just the other day—I can't remember. Hell, yeah, I'm always digging up old Mao quotes and shit, from Mao on contradictions. And also, you know, I also have to be really honest. This is where I do think that some of the shit pops up between Black trade unions and transformative organizing: Mao's stance on matters like metaphysics. Mao would find some of our woo-woo stuff touchy-feely, like Generative Somatics, for example. I haven't done it, but you know, that realm is metaphysics. It's not based on concrete conditions. So, you know, see both sides, but I do check myself, I'm like, am I assessing things through . . . would Mao consider this metaphysical or is this like a real condition that I'm actually assessing? Those are the three that I kind of bump up against a lot in movement work. Making organizing decisions based on our projections on things, but not the concrete.

Do you have any more questions for me?

MF

I was just checking to see. One of the last questions is if there's anything you wanted to bring up that we haven't gone over.

KD

Let me look at your questions. Interpersonal conflict/self-criticism . . . That's a big one. Yeah, definitely practice self-crit. Actually, I think we kind of talked about that.

MF

You definitely touched on it.

KD

Yeah, that for sure is a big part. We definitely practice that in Critical Resistance. We do it every day. I just think it's a good way of life, you know? In movements, yes, but just it's a good way of life, a good way of living—not trying to seek out vengeance in justice and making myself have to be right all the fucking time, you know? I learned a whole lot more just listening and stepping back than I have writing the angry email and having to lash out, even though I've definitely done that. But, you know, I've had really good elders, and good movement folks would be like, "What are you trying to build?" And I feel like that's what we need a lot more, just having that call-in out of love, like, "What are we trying to build?"

MF

That's a really interesting point. That's where you would counsel other younger, greener . . .

KD

Yeah, OK, you're right. But what are you trying to build? A whole mountain where you're right? OK, cool, I'll go visit sometime. But yeah, it's having to have my say is . . . It's not sexy. I don't want to build that.

MF

Sure.

KD

I want gay communists.

MF

That's what we're trying to build.

KD

Yeah, awesome. I want to learn more about Pinko. It's online?

MF

Yeah, it's pinko.online.

KD

I found it. Communism for fags. Yeah, cool. I love it.

MF

That's so kind of you. Sorry I guess we could have gone over this in the beginning. So you and Michelle knew each other from Freedom Road?

KD

Yeah. I was in Florida when I first met Michelle back in like 2008 or 2009? It all blends together. I don't know. And then I moved to New York six years ago, and Michelle was in the district that I joined here in New York. We were in the same district. Michelle was always involved in cool shit. She's one of these people I'm like, "I'm gonna see what Michelle does." So one of them was with the International Women's Strike. At first, I just sort of came to meetings because they had good snacks, and then there were a couple of people I was like, "These people are cool and the politics are cool." But, you know, it's really about the people and the snacks. So then I got involved in that. And then I edited some oral history for the Trans Oral History Project. I did one or two edits. And then we lived in the same neighborhood, I think we still do. We lost touch for a little bit. We were walking buddies, and then I had surgery, so it's been a year, but I could depend on it. That's how we know each other.

MF

So, it's been a series of political collaborations, basically?

KD

As we do, yeah.

MF

And sorry, I know you already mentioned, if I rewind I'll be able to answer this myself, but you got involved with Freedom Road through the workers at UNC?

KD

UNC–Chapel Hill. The housekeepers and groundskeepers. They formed the . . . Well, now it's the North Carolina Public Service Workers Union, UE Local 150. And it was the Black Workers for Justice who are the organization that helped fuel that organizing and the center, and then behind Black Workers for Justice was Black cadre from Freedom Road. And Freedom

Road changed its name last year to Liberation Road. But yeah, that's the trajectory. It took me a long time. As a young person, I was like, "Wait, how do you . . . ? Why is there a socialist organization backing this?" I didn't get it because I didn't live through the Red Scare and all of the blacklisting. And also just how the work happens is through mass organizing. So I didn't get the mass organization Black Workers for Justice and the vanguard of that.

MF

Yeah. But ultimately you did join them?

KD

Yeah, I did. I joined in my mid-twenties when I was still in North Carolina, and then, around 2004, I moved from North Carolina to Florida. I helped create a Liberation Road chapter there, the Freedom Road chapter there. And then we came to New York. Yeah, that's been my trajectory as a communist. I was also an editor for Organizing Upgrade and my heart wasn't into it. I did it because partly because Freedom Road needed somebody on there. I'm like, OK, these people are cool, I'll do it. But my heart right now is doing grad school and just getting through that. It's been my love and, you know, I always wanted to go to seminary. So doing that and going to school, that and being at work, it's like, I just can't even join a Zoom.

Stevie
Wilson

Stevie Wilson is a currently imprisoned Black queer
abolitionist writer and organizer in Pennsylvania.
His political activity began in his teens as the
vice president of a Boston queer youth alliance.
In Philadelphia, he founded queer activist
organizations, participated in the ballroom
scene, and was mentored by local grassroots AIDS
organizers. He now leads abolitionist study groups
in the facilities where he is incarcerated and
publishes the journal *In the Belly*.

STEVIE WILSON

My name is Stevie Wilson. I am a currently imprisoned Black
queer abolitionist writer and organizer.

Accountability, to me, connotes responsibility and healing
in a communal context.

I am Black so I feel that some part of me has always been
in a struggle here in America. Growing up poor and Black, my
life was supposed to be circumscribed by these markers. Being
queer is what made my struggle so much more public. As a teen,
I joined Boston Alliance of Gay and Lesbian Youth (BAGLY),
eventually becoming vice president. It was during my time
with BAGLY that I became an activist. It was the early '90s and
we were raising awareness regarding queer youth suicide and
homelessness. We were highlighting bullying in schools. And
here we are thirty years later and still tackling these issues!

In '93, I came to Philly for college and immediately dove
into the queer activist scene. I was experienced so I was called
upon by different organizations to speak to different audiences,
sometimes schools and other times community groups. I was
one of the founding youth of The Attic [Youth Center] and of
40 Acres of Change, the queer youth of color group at Colours,
Inc. I was mentored by Tyrone Smith and Hal Carter of Unity,
Inc. And I am a ballroom kid. So activism has been something
I have been part of for decades. It was through Hal and Tyrone
that AIDS activism became part of my life. We know that
communities of color were and continue to be hit hard by HIV.
It was these two men who trained me and taught me so much
about community.

Our biggest obstacles have always been bigotry, ignorance
and lack of funding. We had to make something from nothing
while being told we ain't shit! I have always been a connector,
someone who puts people in touch with resources they need. I
have always been an educator/facilitator too. I still am.

The biggest lessons I carry with me today from the
various struggles and communities I have been part of is the
power and necessity of community.

I am reminded of an analogy I read about the necessity of
community. You could be the best firefighter in the world, but
there is no way you can put that forest fire out alone. You need a
team. Audre Lorde reminds us that without community there is
no liberation.

Another related lesson: center relationships. So often we forget this. We get caught up in the goal, the outcome, and forget the process. Our work is based on connections with other people. Without good relations, the work doesn't get done. And if it does, we often napalm the bridges it took to get to our goal. We screw ourselves. My history has taught me to center relationships, to take care of my blessings.

I don't think we do a good job of practicing accountability as a movement. We are not good at handling conflict either. Too often, groups break up because they didn't have procedures or processes to deal with conflict. We wait until something happens and then try to put a plan together. This is like jumping off a cliff and trying to build your wings on the way down.

We have to get comfortable with uncomfortability. We have to practice conflict resolution before we need it. And this is connected to criticism/self-criticism work. If we made this work a regular part of what we do, we would be able to handle conflicts much better. Why is it so hard for us to struggle with each other? We are struggling against massive systems of oppression every day. So we have it in us to struggle with each other.

I have always been more partial to transformative justice. I feel it does so much more than restorative justice. I know that RJ's roots extend back to Indigenous folks. TJ's roots extend back to communities of color. TJ's approach appeals to me because it focuses on the individual and the community. Everyone has a part to play in the healing. That is major for me. It centers the survivor and brings the community together to heal both parties.

This practice speaks to me because on the ballroom scene we could never rely upon the state to protect us or solve conflicts. We had to do it ourselves. So we were practicing abolition and TJ without knowing we were. I see this frequently. People everywhere are solving problems and conflicts without the state. People are getting their needs met when the state abandons them. And this is being done via community.

In order for accountability to work, you need community. Without it, accountability fails. In order to create community, you need connections, care, and the ability to tolerate uncomfortability. Lastly, I highlight the difference between collectivist and communitarian groups. Collectivist groups ask:

What can you do for the group? Communitarian groups ask:
How can we help you be a better version of yourself and how
can we support you? People are turning away from the former.
Especially once conflict rears its head.

Always,
Stevie

LV

LV lives in Los Angeles. She came up in an
anarchist milieu in the early 2000s, doing
counter-summit organizing and taking part in
convergences. She participated in Bash Back!
when it emerged, first in Chicago and then across
multiple US cities. After having taken part in
many projects and collectives that ended in
interpersonal conflict, she decided to get trained
in mediation herself.

LOU CORNUM

As you know, we're doing this long project to understand accountability in its historical context and how it is understood by people who are using it today. We'll get back to this a lot throughout the interview too, but off the bat what are some things that accountability means to you?

LV

Accountability of course has capitalist connotations as far as referencing something like a ledger, an account of good or bad acts. It has very criminal-justice connotations as well, associated with punishment. Also, when people think of accountability, they picture a struggle session where they have to confess all their crimes and people are going to throw rocks at them and stuff. Let's be honest, it does happen sometimes, maybe not necessarily with the rocks, but also sometimes with rocks and bottles and other things I have witnessed.

There's a ton of negative connotations with the word *accountability*. With mediation and transformative justice, all of that entire field, our language is really clunky and it doesn't really fit, in my opinion, what we're trying to do at all. Accountability is a perfect example of one of those words that has all of these negative connotations. But at the same time, when I'm working with folks in terms of conflict mediation or navigating conflicts, we think about accountability more as a dialogue with the community and a commitment to your comrades, and a commitment to self-critique and working through the issues that have come up and issues of harm that either the person was responsible for or experienced or unintentionally created.

There are all of these different ways that somebody can be in commitment with the community, and that kind of commitment is a part of being a revolutionary. I wish that there was more of that understanding of being a revolutionary, the sitting with conflict. Because in the work that we do, we're working with conflict and harm out in the world and fighting these systems of harm and systems of oppression and advocating for this great revolutionary change that's going to happen. These systems affect our spaces in a similar way, so I think that being conflict-averse in our organizing spaces is a contradiction and it's hypocritical. I also understand the

aversion, of course. Conflict is scary, and it's overwhelming.
Dealing with conflict can be an immense amount of work, and
most people don't have even anywhere near the skills to deal.
That's a part of the design of capitalism, things are structured
such that we aren't handling our conflicts ourselves, and we
have to rely on a third party to mediate them, whether the cops
or the psychiatry system, etc.

To me, accountability is that commitment to dialogue
with yourself and with your comrades and sitting with that and
working through that.

LC

It sounds like you've had a prolonged experience with
different contexts in which accountability is coming up in
political or revolutionary spaces. Could you tell us a bit about
the background of your political work and how you came to
political consciousness and trying to actualize that in the world?

LV

I was radicalized in the 2000s, in the post-antiwar movement,
in a sort of anarchist milieu in the Midwest, Chicago in
particular, Denver, and on the West Coast mostly. I was
living in punk houses and doing a lot of the typical anarchist
projects at the time like mass mobilizations and the counter-
summit work. There were different convergences but also
counter-conventions intervening in the DNC and the RNC,
and intervening in these mass movements. So, Bash Back!
came out of that context. And that was a group that I was very
involved in, in the late 2000s. And I definitely think that that
informed a lot of how I understand conflict. Bash Back! was a
short-lived movement, from 2007 to 2008 until basically 2010,
with some post–Bash Back! projects I was also working with,
such as queer militant initiatives. Bash Back!, especially in the
late 2000s, was a very singular way of understanding conflict in
terms of basically embracing conflict in this virulent, visceral
way of living and breathing that conflict. Because I think that
there's a militant queer movement that's also anti-fascist that
Bash Back! was of course a part of. But anytime you think about
what queer militancy looks like in the streets, you have to think
about the quotidian acts of covert racism or other forms of
everyday violence, especially transphobic, transmisogynistic

experiences that you might have on the street that are violent. And how can you respond to that? Bash Back! was very much organized around small groups of people that were protecting each other in these different contexts. And with that, there's an understanding of conflict and violence that is a lot more personal, so when it came to other interpersonal conflict among comrades within Bash Back!, the level of intensity was very high as well, just from this context and from this experience. And it was the interpersonal conflict that brought the first iteration of Bash Back! to an end.

We did a convergence last summer [2023], which was a big success, and everyone had a really great time reconnecting, and it was really powerful on a lot of levels. And so that's coming back in a different form. I'm very interested to see how that looks in this context with younger folks. We had a lot of younger folks come to the convergence. It was interesting because the Bash Back! of the late 2000s—there was a bridge, a very clear bridge between the convergence last summer and my experience with that earlier period, especially when it came to conflict. I was doing a lot of conflict mediation at the convergence and it was very much the same story, fourteen years later, but with a whole new group of younger folks that had very different political intuitions. Also, the more things change, the more they stay the same. There were very similar patterns that were really fascinating for me to see.

In between those two experiences, I've also done a lot of anti-police work, Black Lives Matter abolitionist work, and then in a lot of protest groups related to that, different collectives, and, you know, a lot of different sort of initiatives. Not really in the nonprofit side of the abolitionist movement, but connected. I have also done work with unionizing campaigns, recently with this large independent coffee shop in Los Angeles.

I was also part of a very ambitious communist media project—I'm not going to name it, but people will know what it is—that had a very dramatic end. My experiences with that really informed how I think about conflict. After having been in so many different groups and collectives that had run into irreconcilable conflict and ended as a result of that, this media project was the straw that broke the camel's back. I said, "Enough is enough. I have to learn about mediation myself. I can't go into any more projects without having a more robust understanding of how conflict can be navigated in a way that's not so cataclysmic." There's just so much that I learned from that experience and how it was mishandled, how it could have been done a lot better, but also the complexity of that situation.

Once that ended, I also was very involved in the George Floyd uprising, and spent a lot of time in Los Angeles with the Black Unity Camp, which was a hundred-day encampment outside of City Hall in downtown LA. That also formed the basis of a lot of anti-fascist organizing. Black Unity Camp was the kick-starter to a lot of different initiatives that year and the year following and to this day actually. The conflict that I experienced at the encampment was on a scale that I had never experienced before. It was a very volatile space. And I learned a lot about conflict, but it also raised a lot of questions for me that I'm still processing. How do you navigate all of these different crises—psychological crisis, emotional crisis, PTSD kind of things? All of these different aspects of trauma are coming to the forefront in movement spaces, especially in very high-intensity spaces such as the encampment. When things are moving really fast, how do you take time to work through those things? How do you take time to sit down and work on building your emotional capacity to handle conflict while also doing the work and showing up in the street and continuing to fight?

A lot of the work that I've done since then, in the last few years, has been thinking about 2020 and the George Floyd uprising. How could we have shown up differently in terms of conflict in order to facilitate a more generative experience rather than having this very kind of jagged experience? On the one hand, a lot of conflict was suppressed and avoided, and on the other hand, it would just explode. People would dive into the conflict in a very reckless way, and it would just explode into literal physical fights and bottles being thrown. I'm still trying to learn from that and put into practice what I learn with all of the different collectives and initiatives that I work in currently.

Especially in terms of solidarity with Palestinian resistance, we're seeing a lot of these old stories of conflict and interpersonal stuff. But with the knowledge, especially for me, with trying to incorporate some of the stuff that I've learned over the years in this other context. And I think that it's been really inspiring how, at least in Los Angeles, the folks that I've been working with have been very receptive and very committed to working through these issues. At the same time some of the issues are very difficult. A lot of the accountability work I had done or community accountability or mediation that I had done involved interpersonal harm where there's very clear survivors and harmdoers and rapists, and with that we're navigating community accountability and trying to repair that very clear harm. This is different than in a collective where there are broader instances of racist microaggressions and anti-Blackness. There are instances of harm and instances of interpersonal violence—at the same time, those situations call for clarity that is different from other forms of interpersonal violence because it takes more of a political-education model.

LC

What you described about 2020 and the George Floyd uprising and immediate aftermath, I was thinking that word right before you said it: *explode*. That was also happening in the political spaces in New York City for sure, along with suppression and avoidance. The fallout from that is something that many of us are still processing and haven't really fully addressed or incorporated into different practices.

LV

With comparing to the current Palestinian solidarity movement, there's such a difference in approach. Both the kind of conflict that I experienced in Bash Back! as well as in like the George Floyd uprising. It was very much leaning into this conflict and saying, "If it turns violent then so be it." That's part of conflict mediation, not being afraid of allowing things to bubble over. But in a way that's like, "No, we're not going to kill each other." Sometimes people do need to fight, within reason. I think at least my window into the Palestinian solidarity movement right now, you know, in Los Angeles and the US—the limits of that view need to be considered, it has involved people who are not as accustomed to getting so down and dirty with conflict. There's people like, "Oh no, you're saying something that's more aggressive than I'm used to and that makes me feel unsafe." As mediators, even as we don't want people to feel unsafe, of course, at the same time we don't want people to be policing all the ways other people approach conflict. How do we merge these sensibilities?

The very hands-on mode of navigating conflict, it's not necessarily more efficacious. It doesn't necessarily work better. But it's always better to deal with conflict than it is to avoid it. And so that I will say for this more hands-on approach. I really don't like the term *mediation*. It ends up becoming really cumbersome. Whenever I bring it up, people picture a legal structure with two parties and those parties are going through arbitration. And there's a judge. And the judge is like, instead of being like an accountability facilitator or a mediation facilitator, which is more how we like to structure it. As many times as you say, "We're not arbitrating this, we're facilitating the community's understanding of this conflict," as much as you say that, people still see you as the arbitrator. It's because of all of these frameworks and mediation is a part of that too.

LC

I'd like to hear more about mediation. But first I wanted to go back a bit to thinking about the emergence of Bash Back! and focus in on that formation. It was interesting the way you described it coming out of or following from these large antiwar demonstrations and other mass mobilizations from late '90s through the aughts. Could you speak a little more about what the origins of Bash Back! were as well as the impact of it, for people who might not be as familiar?

LV

The anti-globalization movement, that mode of organizing fed into the antiwar movement in a lot of ways. Then the post-antiwar movement was a kind of convergence-hopping, which also had the counter-summit thing going on while also disrupting these large conventions. Bash Back! was definitely within that milieu and also a reaction to that. We had noticed that a lot of these radical scenes in a lot of different US cities ended up becoming controlled by what my comrade calls "philosopher kings." The bros that have consolidated power. Anarchism is very conducive to power consolidation. Everything is all whisper networks, and you can't call anybody out for being an authoritarian because oh, no, nobody's an authoritarian, and all of this kind of stuff. There's all this power consolidation around straight-white-male anti-identity politics, like suppression of survivors, suppression of people that call out homophobia, transphobia in the movement, and suppression of any critique of that. There were definitely two movements in response to this: one was more of a feminist, survivor, anti-rape movement that I feel was embodied by the "We'll Show You Crazy Bitches" type of communiqués and stuff that happened in New York. There were a lot of different feminist initiatives that weren't as flashy that were happening all around the country and world at that time. Then Bash Back! at the same time, we were ******* sick of these men that are controlling everything and just strangling our ability to exist and organize. That was the origin of Bash Back!

A couple of years ago, a lot of my Bash Back! comrades, when we started to see the resurgence of Save the Family and fascist, anti-LGBT stuff, we were asking, "Where are our radical peers?" We looked at the patterns and we said, "Oh, the same thing is happening right now that was happening around 2008, where these philosopher kings, these men, are dominating the radical scene and basically protecting abusers in a whole variety of different contexts and exiling and suppressing survivors, exiling and suppressing trans people, queer people, people of color, anybody that brings up anything that's disrupting this power structure." So, Bash Back! was reanimating itself recently in a similar critical context to its beginnings.

LC

You'd said that there's also something pretty singular about Bash Back!—how so? I'd also like to hear more about what some of the lessons from that struggle are that are relevant to others.

LV

When I was saying that it was singular, I was meaning in terms of the approach to conflict. It's just embedded in "Bash Back" as a slogan. It's a particular way, a very in-your-face way of dealing with conflict. I'm going to come back at you. Whatever you throw at me, I'm going to send back your way, basically. As much as that speaks to a radical sensibility in terms of mass movement and mass organizing in the street, saying, "We're not going to just stand there and let these fascists beat us up," or "We're not going to just cower and let fascists take over our cities for these horrifying rallies that they're doing. We're going to stand up and we're going to fight that." There's a mass movement sensibility to that, but there's also an interpersonal side of it. I think that approach to conflict is fairly unique in terms of other movements. There're many other movements that I've been involved in that have people that approach conflict in that way, in a very hands-on, in-your-face way. Especially in 2020, that was a prevalent sensibility. But to have a whole movement structured around that, like Bash Back! is, is a pretty unique approach.

The result of that is that at the convergence last year—it was maybe because I was working so much on mediation—it felt like everybody was talking about how we deal with conflict and how conflict is navigated and theorizing about the different ways that people believe that conflict should be handled and should be dealt with. There are all sorts of different varieties of political approaches to that. There's what I would consider more of a communist approach, which is very methodical and structured when this conflict comes to us. Obviously, we're not disavowing any sort of in-your-face acts. If people need transformative justice and mediation, we are always emphasizing there are consequences. We especially tell harm-doers, there are consequences to your actions and a lot of times those consequences are violent, and you need to be aware that this is a possibility. When you cause harm, those consequences will come back at you. As much as there's that awareness of the possibility for more intense confrontations, this approach is definitely more of the approach of harm reduction. It's conflict harm reduction. Where we're going to work through this, we're going to talk about it. This is within the Bash Back! tradition and other approaches to conflict with movement spaces. A lot of my learning about this comes from Black Liberation, Black understandings of abolitionism, and all sorts of different movements. Especially the Creative Interventions Toolkit ["A Practical Guide to Stop Interpersonal Violence"] and a number of other theorists inform me.

There's a social-mapping process that happens with mediation where the two parties have a rupture between them. In order to navigate that rupture, you have to take more of a bird's-eye view and think about the people that are surrounding them. And think about common values that are shared between their larger social circles. Sometimes those larger social circles aren't enough, and you have to take an even higher bird's-eye view and approach it from even larger social-mapping formations and all of that. All of that kind of work takes a lot of emotional energy, and a lot of it just takes a lot of time, literal hours having conversations with each of the people who are involved and especially the secondary and then the tertiary people that are involved in that. And then thinking about the folks on the other side of the conflict and then going back to the original party, and there's a lot of back and forth.

The biggest problem when it comes to mediating in these spaces is burnout and finding capacity to work through all of that stuff. I'm happy to talk more about that structure, but all of that to say I think that's more what I would consider a communist approach. You could call it an anarchist approach too, of course. It's embracing this methodical way of handling conflict and sitting with that.

There's also more of the nihilist approach or the insurrectionary approach, anarcho-insurrectionary, but what I've noticed is that people are less identifying as an anarcho-insurrectionist and more saying, "I'm just nihilist now." Especially with younger comrades. That's at least the way that I'm noticing that. So, the nihilist approach is more when people are doing the "braver spaces" kind of things. That's another approach to conflict that people are using at different convergences now. That's more, like, whatever happens, happens; nobody's going to stop anything from happening. People will get involved if people are getting in a fight and it is getting out of control; people will probably jump in and try to separate people. But nobody's going to sit at the table and come to any resolution. They're trying to escalate hostilities and want to live in this kind of perpetual warfare. Obviously, you can probably tell it's not exactly my approach. I have come to have a lot of love and respect for my nihilist comrades, and I adore them in a lot of ways, and I also disagree with them in this regard a lot. At the same time, I think Bash Back! is really interesting because it's a space that literally has to hold both of those traditions at the same time. Not only that, but even though there are two separate traditions, nobody fully embodies one tradition or the other.

I don't even necessarily believe in political identities, because identities are so malleable, and we're just these complicated social creatures that are swimming through all of these different settings. To say that somebody is a pure nihilist or a pure communist or a pure anarchist or whatever just doesn't resonate with my experience with people. Bash Back! has to hold these two different currents at the same time and people are dancing between the two of them. It has a lot to say in terms of conflict resolution and navigating conflict when you are embracing this in-your-face version and also trying to have the more harm-reduction style of conflict resolution and mediation.

LC

So, there's largely two tendencies, a more communist-anarchist tendency and another nihilist, and these each have their attendant orientation toward conflict, with a mediation-focused process on one hand and, a term I wasn't familiar with, "braver spaces" on the other. Does that correlate to what you were laying out?

LV

Right, "braver spaces" is a kind of shorthand for more of a hands-off nihilist approach, where there are no boundaries to how people respond to conflict and so no boundary to where violence could occur. At Bash Back! '23 we had a whole discourse in the lead-up around whether or not it was OK for someone to mace someone they had a disagreement with in an indoor space. It may sound ludicrous, but the "braver spaces" advocates (nihilists) were really adamant that [we] would tread on their rights to not let them mace indoors. Of course, we put our foot down, because we weren't going to do anything to attract police attention and the fact that a lot of people could have health issues if they got secondhand maced. But "braver spaces" would be on the pro–macing indoors side of that "debate."

LC

So, is there a set of formal practices within Bash Back! for addressing interpersonal conflict? Or does it depend on the different geographic context? Are there different chapters where a different orientation has more sway over a specific chapter than others?

In the new iteration of Bash Back!, there's no real kind of
formal anything. Everything's very informal. And I think that
the legacy of Bash Back! is that more people are more averse
to any sort of formal structure than other groups or other
movements that I've been involved in. I don't really see Bash
Back! coming up with a formal approach to conflict even though
personally I wouldn't be opposed to it. I know that the vast
majority of my comrades in Bash Back! would be very opposed
to it, so I have a hard time seeing that come to fruition. But at the
same time, I do think that having resources around mediation,
such as zines and other publications that help people to navigate
that, is a part of Bash Back!.

So, for the convergence last summer, for that space we
had a particular approach to conflict that I had worked out with
some comrades, obviously in dialogue with everybody that was
participating in the convergence. We were not imposing anything
on anybody, instead basically offering the space to be: "Look, me
and a number of comrades are going to organize ourselves in a
way that is available to people that want to approach conflict in
this more structured way. If you want that and if you don't, then
obviously you can go about it in your own way." And people did.

The Bash Back! Convergence, at least in my circles, was
the first large convergence that people had been to in many years.
Maybe even a decade, but definitely since the pandemic. Now
we're seeing the convergences in Tucson and convergences in
Pittsburgh and other cities. A lot of especially younger folks,
but also a lot of us that were going to that convergence hadn't
really been in proximity with each other for quite a while. A
lot of backlog conflicts were coming to the forefront. People
were walking around the corner and getting into arguments and
punching each other and then getting over it and then walking
back to the convergence, holding hands. And then going and
getting into arguments with Maoists. That's how one conflict
was resolved. We all were saying, "OK, that's a beautiful way of
dealing with your conflict." And then there was all of these other
ways that conflict was resolved. We were helping folks to navigate
a lot of that stuff, and some worked better than others.

That was for the national convergence last summer in
Chicago, and for this summer, there are going to be more
regional convergences. There's a number that have been called

for, that have been called in different cities: Philly, the Pacific Northwest . . . . There's another one in Oregon. I can't keep track of all of them. There's a number of regional gatherings and all of those gatherings are going to approach conflict in their own ways. I was talking with some of the folks at Philly about our approach to conflict in Chicago. They're going to have to figure it out on their own. I would like to have a bigger initiative of comrades that are working in this vein across different cities. A lot of this conflict can be also done through phone calls or through video chats and different things like that, so you don't necessarily need to be in the same city. It would be great to have a network of people that are interested in this and willing to put in the time to help navigate this stuff for and within radical movement spaces. We're not really there. There's talk about something like that, and we talked about it last summer, but there's a lot of work to be done to bring that into reality.

LC

Earlier you invoked the work of harm reduction as an approach to conflict—this is somewhat unique compared to others we've spoken to. I'm wondering if there are other related conflict concepts or practices and traditions that Bash Back! has engaged with such as accountability processes, transformative justice, restorative justice, or, speaking of the Maoists, criticism/self-criticism?

LV

I would definitely say that all of those, maybe minus the Maoist approach, all of those are used within Bash Back! I think that for anybody that's approaching conflict, there are always unique situations, because it involves asking someone that has caused harm to grow.

All of the conflict handled in Bash Back! is done through an abolitionist transformative justice modality. That's a given. Because it is striving to be as noncarceral as possible, and it's also striving to create space for personal growth. Every time you ask somebody to grow or you give them the opportunity to grow, they are going to grow in their own unique way. And people that have been harmed are going to need a wide variety of different things. Justice is going to look like a lot of different things.

What I've noticed in the spaces that I've worked in, folks are very adverse to accountability processes, which I find very interesting. I've asked people for articles, resources, and zines that they're looking at. Because there's so many people that are like, "Oh, accountability processes are neoliberal identity politics." Like *enclosure* or all these buzzwords that people throw at me. I want to read what they're reading so I can understand where they're coming from with this. I understand the downside of formal accountability processes, of course. They can be manipulated and used in a lot of cynical, bad-faith ways. I saw that in so many different contexts. I've seen that as soon as you create a formal process, the first thing that somebody is going to do is abuse that process to do something that's out of step with the values of the groups. I understand the hesitancy around formal accountability process, basically where a group is like, "If somebody does this, then this is what's going to happen." That's codifying like a legal document and codifying a mode of behavior. Communists are, of course, a little friendlier to that. Even though most of the communists that I work with are very adverse to that kind of approach to conflict. But anarchists are especially adverse to it, and nihilists won't touch it with a ten-foot pole.

Formal accountability processes are, as far as I'm concerned, dead in the water. It does feel like something out of the '90s and I can think of a lot of resources that were like, "This is how you do the accountability process, blah blah." What I find in everything that I read about conflict, especially in the Creative Interventions Toolkit and other resources, is that there's not a one-size-fits-all approach to accountability.

The process that you go through to understand accountability is actually just a social process of having conversations with a lot of different people and creating space for folks to come to their own understanding. The way that I do mediation and the way that I organize mediation in Bash Back! and in other contexts is to emphasize: We are facilitators. And this is straight from the Creative Interventions Toolkit. Yes, we're mediators, but people get hung up on the term *mediation*. *Facilitation* is a lot better of a term. We're facilitating this conversation between these different groups. As facilitators, at the end of this process, we're not going to say, "This one person needs to do X, Y, and Z, and this person needs to do X, Y, Z," or "We're going to exile this person and that's the best thing for the group." That's not the role of the facilitators. The role of the facilitators is simply to be in this very engaged and communicative space where you're having dialogue with all these different people. Sometimes at the end of that, that will result in writing something, writing your understanding, as facilitators, of a conflict. That writing isn't necessarily public. It's more like a letter that you might write to an organizing collective or to a couple of other people. It's still within this dialogical process. When I think about the accountability process, that's what I think about, a dialogical process.

But people get very hung up on the terms. How can we frame that in a way that's more understandable to our comrades without scaring them off with all of this terminology? Harm reduction is maybe a way to frame it that's a little more palatable for people and also explains it maybe a little bit better. What I find is that a big part of mediation is the very initial ask for people to work through their conflict. That's literally fifty-fifty whether or not you're going to succeed. So, say there's a conflict that comes up with two people, and what happens is one of the parties is going to come to you or you're going to talk with them. Generally, one of the parties is going to come to you and say, "I want mediation. I want this solved. I want justice. X, Y, Z." Maybe they've been harmed or maybe there's an abuser in their midst. Or maybe it's a small interpersonal thing going on. But that one party is pretty enthusiastic about going through something. Then the second party, from what I've experienced, is generally going to be like, "Oh, I don't think that this is a conflict. I don't think that I need to deal with this. I don't need mediation, and I certainly am not going to go through an accountability process. I don't want anything to do with any of that."

As the mediator, or as the facilitator, the first thing that you've got to do is have a very meandering, somewhat gentle conversation with the second party where you explain what the process is and tell them, "We're not dictating your behavior." Hopefully they're part of the radical movement and see themselves as a dedicated comrade to the struggle. Then you can be like, "We want to facilitate making your experience in this group better. If you cause harm, obviously any good comrade wants to rectify that harm that they cause, and they don't want to be out there causing harm." You have to be very persuasive, essentially, not manipulating anybody but you have to be very cautious with the terminology.

We have no tools. And this is 100 percent capitalist design, this is proceeding according to the plan of capitalism. I feel like we're stuck in the Stone Age when it comes to conflict. These situations are so nuanced, so delicate, and we have one sledgehammer. And we're trying to use the sledgehammer very delicately. That's how I see all of our terminology. *Accountability* is like a sledgehammer of a term. And the accountability process is like a giant boulder that you push off a cliff with somebody standing beneath it. That's the way that people see it. All of these terms are just so heavy and so loaded. We have yet to develop enough of a nuanced understanding of conflict, interpersonal conflict, to handle these things with precision and grace.

Then the other side of it is that literally nobody wants to do the work. It always falls on the same people, who are generally femmes. It's also racialized. So, a lot of that work falls on femmes of color. It's all the same story about this work that needs to be done. Nobody wants to do it. Who's going to pick up the pieces and actually do this work? The people that end up doing this work, with the structure that I was talking about in terms of taking the bird's-eye view and talking with all the different people, it takes dozens and dozens of hours to address a simple conflict. In a complicated conflict, it's going to take a lot longer. Who has time for all of that? You want to spread it out among a number of different people, but as soon as you do that, then the question of training comes in. If you bring the wrong person into the process, then they're going to make everything worse. Then you're talking about how to get everybody trained up in order to have these conversations. It's just knowing how to do active listening, knowing the role, and having some grounding. You don't have to be a super expert or anything to do the work, but you do have to have some training. Any sort of training takes more capacity and more hours.

At this point, every collective that I enter into, every movement space that I enter into, I try to tell people we need to approach conflict in the same way that we approach food or feeding massive groups of people. If our groups are dozens of people or up to a couple of hundred people, then think about what it takes to feed all of those people. It takes chefs, it takes procuring all of that food, it takes having the right tools to cook that food, and then you have to have the means, the space to serve the food. That process we all understand from all of our experience with cooking for either parties or large groups of people at protests or protest encampments or other situations of serving large groups of people. We understand how complicated it is and how much work goes into it. We have to approach conflict in that exact same way, with that same rigor. Thinking about all of the different components that it takes to solve conflict is as complicated and takes as much resources as it would to feed people. I don't think that we're even close to being able to handle conflict at that level.

But I do think that more and more people are moving in that direction. Conversations are being had. People are more open to it. They're more receptive to all of this work. They're learning a lot more. There's a lot better understanding, especially with younger comrades. They have a much better understanding of conflict and emotional capacity and all of the things that it takes to navigate this stuff than any other generation. I'm optimistic that we'll get there.

LC

That's an amazing comparison between provision of food and thinking about conflict in that way. Is there anything that we haven't talked about yet that you want to make sure to address or emphasize before we end?

LV

I think the biggest problem that we face in movement spaces and in the radical community is conflict avoidance. There's a lot to be said about the origins of conflict avoidance. If I was a writer, I would probably sit down and write out some of my thoughts on this. I think that conflict avoidance is definitely connected with all of the systems of oppression that we face. I think it's absolutely a part of whiteness and it's patriarchy and it's part of bourgeois domination. People obviously have trauma responses to conflict, and I'm not really talking about that. Of course, some are going to say, "Oh, I'm conflict-averse because of my trauma." But let's be honest, conflict aversion is built into the framework of our society. So, when it comes to radical communities, it's the exact same patterns. People are very afraid to go down that road with conflict. There's a lot of supposedly "common sense" intuitions around conflict suppression. I see a lot, just to be frank, I see this with the

Tiqquinists; out of all of the communities I've interfaced with, they are the worst when it comes to that kind of attitude towards conflict. I think it's also because they're very much openly into all of the individualistic anti-identity politics, they don't want to talk about their whiteness or their patriarchy, or how all of their structures of power circle around that. I think their work is the poster child of conflict avoidance in radical spaces. But it's also a part of all of our spaces.

I think the first step to creating communities that have healthy ways of dealing with conflict and generative ways. . . That's the other thing that I really firmly believe about conflict is that it can be generative. I wish that I could just make an easy slogan like that, "Conflict is generative," but I think we all know that there's so many examples of it not being generative at all. But I do think that conflict has the possibility of being extremely generative. I think that even interpersonal conflict, even instances of harm, even instances of sexual violence among comrades—all of these instances can be generative if they're handled in the right way. I'm not saying that that means that rapists need to be embraced in all of our spaces. Or that survivors have to share spaces with their abusers. I'm not saying that at all, but I am saying that in the process of handling conflict, I've noticed that when it's done right, it's always generative, and that's kind of a beautiful and amazing side of things. It's actually a power that we can harness if we organize ourselves in a way that can handle the capacity that it takes to navigate conflict in a healthy way.

LC

I really appreciate the breadth of everything that you've experienced but also interpreted and analyzed. It resonates a lot with aspects I've been troubled by, particularly with structural conflict aversion.

LV

Thank you so much for the opportunity to talk about it. I feel that there needs to be more work out there about conflict avoidance. That's one of the biggest things that we're not talking about, and it's embedded in everything that we do. And it fucks everything up.

"COMMUNITY?
WHAT
COMMUNITY?"

Analyzing the Limits of Account ability

ACCOUNTABILITY
TRADITIONS
VARIED MEANINGS
THE EROTIC
FAILURES

COMMUNITY
PRECARITY OF COMMUNITY
COMMUNITY OF CAPITAL
FANTASY OF COMMUNITY
ABOLITION
ASPIRATIONS OF COMMUNITY

This volume collects many brilliant and important organizers, grappling with questions of accountability from quite varied perspectives. Each interview, in its own ways, offers considerable material for everyone trying to find better approaches to addressing intra-movement harm. But this book is not quite a manual or collection of best practices, nor is it a programmatic guide for what we think others should be doing differently.

Essential to this project are the tensions and contradictions between interviews. In the introduction, we named what we saw as an impasse in current debates on accountability, a set of intractable contradictions in debates on the topic. Overcoming this impasse will likely depend on a further advance in the streets, in the conditions of mass struggle. We hope that through placing these differing conversations alongside each other, something more can begin to emerge dialectically that would be absent in isolation. Since some of these interviews were first circulated in October 2023, we've had the chance to do a series of public events with contributing narrators and audiences. Those have advanced our sense that the questions that brought us to this project are crucial but not yet fully answered. This book is an effort to open up new trajectories of thinking and working between and through the tensions of these interviews.

For this conclusion, rather than closely engage the rich material of the interviews, we are setting out on a lateral trajectory, first in recognizing some of the discursive maneuvers and absences in the interviews, and then in theorizing the limits of accountability through a critique of the capitalist mode of production.

ACCOUNTABILITY

Over the last decade, a specific framework for addressing intra-movement harm has become dominant. In its rigorous form, it is often called transformative justice (TJ). TJ has spread with the growing prominence of prison and police abolitionism and with a few high-profile and brilliant advocates. It has been taken up by many activists seeking the best available practices for addressing and repairing harms between members of a shared community. Some imagine TJ as replacing the prison-industrial complex, growing to become a primary means of addressing all forms of interpersonal harm. Already, many politically savvy people consider it the go-to standard for managing sexual abuse within movement space.

Central to transformative justice is a recognition of the destructive violence of the capitalist, white-supremacist state. For communities targeted by mass incarceration, police violence, and criminalization, calling on the police and courts is often unviable. Through groups like INCITE!, feminists of color played a major role in developing transformative justice as a framework. Their experience of simultaneously challenging police violence and intimate-partner violence made clear the necessity of other frameworks for addressing harm. Those organizing against police and prisons are particularly drawn to transformative justice as a framework.

While TJ is a fairly specific set of overlapping practices, it has also inspired a more vague and expansive approach to movement harm, often termed *accountability*. "Holding an abuser accountable," "an ongoing accountability process," "a failed effort at accountability," "being accountable to survivors"—these phrases and others like them circulate among social networks online, are taken up in conflict-ridden organizing meetings, and form the quiet gossip that constitutes many relationships between comrades when protest isn't popping off.

They are both quite specific and quite general. They are specific in the sense that their meanings are not necessarily intelligible to those outside movement spaces, or from other generations of activists. Even the language of "harm" as encompassing manifold forms of violence and conflict belongs to a particular historical and cultural moment. Those using these phrases mark themselves as part of a specific set of milieus, a particular age range, and a few overlapping movements or the broader social networks and discursive communities around such movements. These phrases are laden with moral weight, with the accumulated baggage of experiences of pain and betrayal.

Ideas of accountability are also general in the sense that what exactly constitutes an accountability process is rarely clear, far from standardized, and constantly subject to contestation and debate. Some define accountability entirely in terms of the desire and needs of survivors. Others frame it as primarily driven by a community's needs, by a shared or collective will. Some see accountability as a formal, clear-cut process with steps and set expectations. Others relate to it as an open-ended political confrontation, a public struggle over what sorts of behaviors are tolerated among comrades; they may consider accountability as a weapon to challenge oppressive power dynamics within movements. Some see accountability as a means of disciplining harmful behavior through imposed consequences, while others are wary of anything that suggests a logic of punishment. Some are willing to use coercion, like deplatforming, to force perpetrators to participate in an accountability process, while others see mutual consent and mutual willingness as essential for a functional process.

Accountability can be a principled moral stance, a nebulous but inspired political vision of loving movements, a commitment to ending and transforming harm within our movement spaces. Its promise is great: that movements can wage our struggles against police or capital or fascists, while within our ranks finding ways to care for each other, heal our trauma, and prefigure a world beyond prisons and courts. We can imagine success: survivors feeling protected and cared for; processes leading to substantial transformation in behavior; projects that could continue to move ahead in broader struggles, armed with a sustained internal culture that could mitigate, stop, and redress harm. Accountability is a promise to commit ourselves to transforming and learning from each other, to becoming better comrades.

TRADITIONS

What we call the queer left is less a movement or a community than a hodgepodge of traditions made from transmitted inheritances of the politics and practices of those who struggled before us.

In the absence of an actually existing community, all we have is the community that harms us and through which we must seek repair. Searching for continuity, but skeptical of normative institutions, the queer left looks to a sense of tradition—a somewhat stable repertoire of ethical practices that bind people together in common cause. In seeking an unproblematic authority from which to claim their own traditions, many well-meaning queers have turned toward an Indigenous past as their wellspring of inspiration and intention, one that marks a kind of prelapsarian vision of another way to live. This is the recurring dream of primitive communism: a way to talk about communism without naming communism. A wish image drawn from a past reality not understood on its own terms but reanimated for transformation of the present. It's not as exaggerated a form as playing Indian; it is more respectful than that. It may be genuine, though it is also instrumentalizing. It is a kind of mythmaking.

This mythic time obscures historical time. Romantic attachment to ideas of Indigenous practices also obscures how current-day practices of reparative justice for Indigenous peoples in Canada and New Zealand often exist within and alongside the colonial government's legal system. Even when not operating through state institutions, Indigenous community practices to address harm do not always align with the values and politics ascribed to them by non-Indigenous proponents citing these traditions. Indigenous communities have used a variety of activities to address harm that may not be palatable or even possible for the proponents who cite them, including exile and intensive ceremonial practices, and which to properly carry out would require restoring Indigenous sovereignty over land. The recursive mention of Indigenous forms of reparative justice is one attempt to ground accountability in its concrete history, which draws from a multitude of precedents transmitted through a structure of feeling more often than through an explicit continuous political program.

It was this project's intention to restore that concrete sense of history to practices of accountability. Not to say that our forms of accountability have gotten any better or worse. It is certainly possible that contemporary practices to address harm are shaped by the vast, varied practices of peoples living across the American continent prior to European arrival. But there are numerous other antecedents, and much more direct influences, on how we have come to consider and mobilize accountability. We began this investigation considering one hypothetical antecedent—the New Communist Movement's influence on contemporary organizing—but found that many narrators emphasized their differences more than their commonalities or a direct lineage. Other potential lineages emerged in the course of our interviews that could have provided alternative research paths. One rich vein of theoretical and practical activity at work in the concept of accountability is the Black radical tradition; in the introduction we pointed to political-prisoner struggles and organizing against intimate-partner violence as two such relevant histories. All share the fact of a non-mythic history of the concept.

VARIED MEANINGS

When we interviewed people about accountability, it quickly became clear that they interpreted the term in varied ways. At first many older comrades primarily spoke about their own efforts to remain accountable to a broader movement and struggle, and the particular political commitments that movement calls on. As people age, see the waning of waves of struggle, and have to reproduce themselves amid the demands of labor markets and institutions, there is considerable pressure to drift away from political activity. To remain accountable is to keep these commitments, even when they are hard and inconvenient.

In our extended political networks, people sometimes talk about accountability as an essential dimension of all camaraderie. We are accountable to each other in the sense that we are ready to fight alongside each other, fight *for* each other, and work through what comes up to maintain viable collaborative relationships. Accountability, in this sense, is a synonym or dimension of solidarity: *I am accountable to you because I recognize we are in this struggle together and have to take care of each other.*

All these meanings—to be accountable to address harm, accountable to a movement, accountable to a comrade—are contrasting but also interconnected. They all are about a commitment to positioning ourselves in a particular way with respect to one another, and about a form of internalized discipline according to which one takes in the desires and needs of the other and makes them a part of oneself. An accountability process may try to force someone to agree to such a discipline, but the taking in and taking on for of accountability for oneself is always an essential step. Accountability is about ourselves as relational beings, open to the desire of others.

THE EROTIC

We go to meetings to cruise. There is work to be done, of course, and many good reasons to do it. We have a protest to plan, a march to coordinate, an arrested comrade to defend, a revolution for which we want to be ready. We also show up for other, more visceral pleasures. We flirt across the room, exchange numbers. When sex isn't what we are seeking, that same erotic tension sublimates into the excitement over a new friend. Some of us met our long-term partners at meetings. We all have a long list of exes and friends accumulated from years of political engagement.

When a protest wave dies down, the erotic is still woven in with the political. We develop a crush on someone we haven't met from reading their excellent and incisive essay, reflecting philosophically on the limits of police reform. The erotic weaves through political action. Queer struggle has been fueled and sustained by the passionate attachments between comrades.

These attractions can also go horribly wrong. Dear friends have been raped by someone we thought was a comrade. Some boyfriends turned violent and controlling a few months in, and it takes years for us to get out. Alcohol and bad social codes blur the lines between miscommunicators and predators. Where there are exes, there are also enemies. And our enemies have allies, splitting organizations and scenes. We keep lists in our heads of bad dates, bad organizations who defend them, bad activists who harass and terrorize survivors. Sexual assault leaves survivors traumatized. It also leaves movements wrecked by betrayal and denial.

Sexual violence occupies a unique place in the litany of interpersonal harms. Sometimes people point this out critically, as if it shouldn't be the case. There are many ways we are oppressed, many ways to become traumatized, and many structures of power and domination. But something in sex goes deep into our being. The erotic is appealing precisely because it has the potential to touch us at our most vulnerable. Desire opens us to the world, and that openness inflects and intensifies the experience of betrayal and harm. And desire isn't always for the good, the safe, the harmless. Much of kink includes a fantasy experience of powerlessness. Those who say that rape is about power, not about sex, seem to miss that kink is so often sexy because there is a play, however consensual, with powerlessness. The erotic is dangerous, and it can hurt us like nothing else.

Strangely, in our interviews about accountability and intra-movement harm, almost no one acknowledged that people date within movement spaces. Though there is no shortage of stories about challenging rape and intimate-partner violence between comrades, the conversations often veered into other, safer kinds of harm. There is some block to really exploring the basis and consequences of sexual harm. It is hard to talk about. It is hard because it is often where there is the most pain and the most trauma. It is hard because it is marked by a certain intimacy. Sexual harm ruptures the confines of the private and personal. But as it spills into the public, it still bears the mark of a kind of private shame.

It may also be hard to talk about, perhaps, because it isn't easy to untangle the risk of sexual assault with our desires. We wish to find erotic pleasure in movement spaces, to be loved and to love, to be touched and to touch. We want to go to meetings to cruise. When we do, there is the potential for sexual harm that could tear through camaraderie and solidarity, leaving organizations and movements in ruins.

FAILURES

The promise of accountability is rarely kept. Across movement spaces, there are countless examples of failed accountability efforts. People try to hold each other to account, and so very many things go wrong.

In the face of accountability efforts, perpetrators may opt out, seeing the process as unreasonable and unnecessary. Supporters of the survivor may recognize they lack the leverage to force an adequate process and start organizing to bring together other allies to pressure the perpetrator into participating. This may take the form of personal interventions, deplatforming, banning them from various spaces, public humiliation, or threatening some aspect of their livelihood and social reproduction. These tactics may hope to force the perpetrator back into a process, or to warn others that this person is dangerous. Supporters of the perpetrator, often with considerably more resources, counter-organize and are frequently successful in forcing survivors to abandon their public life in activist spaces. When at their most determined, accountability efforts may successfully ruin an abuser's reputation or bring an end to a project sustained by denied abuse and repeated cover-ups. More often they lead to splits, entire groups of people remembering their resentments a decade later. Both sound preferable to inaction, no doubt, or to continuing to let abuse and harm circulate. But they are hardly inspiring and enviable outcomes. It is remarkably rare to see examples of intra-movement harm being addressed in ways that were experienced as successful. Instead, the catastrophes and wreckage of failed accountability are everywhere to be found.

So why does this process prove so impossible? An easy response, and one worth sustained attention, is that we need to get better at it. We have models to draw from, experiences to build upon, and brilliant luminaries to listen to. These all are essential, and well-deserving of praise. Pinko's research project into accountability taught us a bit about the lineage and meaning of these concepts. There is much to say about what we learned.

Still, accountability seems difficult to achieve. Something in that difficulty needs to be thought about, something beyond the need for better models, greater efforts, more training. One possible and tentative answer we came to through our own discussions: Accountability processes often fail because they necessarily depend on the existence of what people call "the community." Yet community, far from being something easy to rely on, poses a difficulty of its own.

Both the formalized, transformative justice versions and the vague expansiveness of references to accountability processes make frequent reference to "community." "Community accountability" is a subset of transformative justice, referring to its most common mode of implementation. Mariame Kaba and Shira Hassan titled their transformative justice handbook *Fumbling Towards Repair: A Workbook for Community Accountability Facilitators*. Mia Mingus's online guide on transformative justice contrasts the state, a source of racist harm, with the superior "possibility for transformation in our communities." Generation FIVE includes in their definition of accountability "holding people who commit violence accountable within and by their communities."

Community here is not just a rhetorical device. As attested to by our interviewees and our personal experiences, community is a central mechanism through which accountability processes function. These processes draw on the resources of the community to work effectively, and they may integrate the friends, extended family members, colleagues, and comrades of both a survivor and a perpetrator. These webs of relationships help cohere the process; push perpetrators to participate; support survivors; and provide the grounding, shared space that makes it all possible. Community can help moderate and mediate the numerous tensions and conflicts of an accountability process. When perpetrators are resistant to participating, community pressure can be an essential tool. Concerned friends may express their moral judgment that the perpetrator should stay with a process. Artistic or political collaborators may threaten to throw them out of collective spaces if they do not. Community is the necessary third term that enables and structures accountability without recourse to the state.

In our interviews, people cited various institutions and scenes that function as a community in this sense. One interviewer described efforts at accountability within a punk music scene. Others referenced the importance of a revolutionary party or structured political organization to support the process. Outside the far left, we've seen many examples of people relying on their church, religious community, or twelve-step program to address harm without the state. Even a fantasy community of political desire can help an accountability process; interviewees comment that if all parties see themselves as part of a shared, overall political effort, accountability can be easier to engage. All these factors underline the function of the community as the third term of accountability, situating participants and enabling their mutual engagement.

Community is the stage and site of accountability. It is the leverage and fulcrum of holding to account. It is the entity that brings together survivor and abuser, participants and organizers, in order to make accountability conceivable. Community is the imagined basis and the hoped-for outcome of accountability. We can hold each other accountable because we are in community together. This dependence on community could help explain recent widespread failures of accountability, the difficulty of consistent implementation, and its frequent disappointments.

In many cases, the success or failure of an effort at accountability clearly rests on political factors in these shared contexts, organizations, or communities. Some political organizations have catastrophically imploded when it became clear their leadership had long covered over sexual harm and actively suppressed efforts to address it. In other cases, prevalent but under-acknowledged misogyny or racism may give abusers disproportionate power to undermine accountability processes. In these sorts of situations, faults in the shared reference point make accountability unlikely to impossible, and transforming those shared spaces would be the necessary foundation to future accountability efforts. Clearly we all need more spaces and groups that are more thoroughly committed in their praxis, that take harm and efforts to address it seriously, that recognize the catastrophic impact of allowing sexual harm to continue particularly in its racialized manifestations. Here we want to point toward another, more difficult possibility: that those shared communities rarely exist as they are imagined, in part due to the material structure of capitalist society.

PRECARITY OF COMMUNITY

Communities struggle to persist and survive against the corrosive forces of labor-market competition, state violence, and the material necessity of survival. They may be profoundly important to us, but they often fail people when in crisis, when in need, and when trying to navigate through the treacherous conditions of working-class survival.

Working-class social life has been dominated either by the fragmentation of poverty, white supremacy, and state violence, or by the autonomization and isolation of suburbs, social isolation, and overwork. The destruction of the community can be tracked across macro levels of urban planning, Indigenous peasant dispossession, mass incarceration, and genocide. Entire neighborhoods can be obliterated over the course of a few years through gentrification and urban redevelopment. Working-class communities, particularly for people of color, are under constant erosive pressure from state policies and capitalist markets.

Often, senses of community are particularly robust for people in their twenties, prior to the full isolating effects of labor-market social reproduction. As we age, we tend to become more isolated, alone, and restricted to a narrow world of work and family. Overlapping social worlds may unravel as people retreat into a more isolated life while raising children, grappling with mental-health challenges, or overworking. People may have to move cities to find a new job, leaving behind family or friends. People are incarcerated, detained, or deported. People may go off to college, to pursue a hoped-for career, or to flee the economic despair of their region of origin. A tight-knit network of friends or comrades may be torn apart by conflict, harm, or drama.

In both macro destruction of whole neighborhoods and personal atomization, the dynamics of capitalist markets and the adjunctive role of the racial state and the nuclear family are central to this destruction of community. Capitalist development systematically undermines and upends stable communities and prevents the long-term stability of new ones. Communities under capitalism are fleeting. As Stevie Wilson put it when discussing prisoner organizing in our introduction, "[G]rowing up, they don't feel a part of their community. They don't feel a part of their neighborhood. You see that a lot of them don't feel part of their family. And then you come to prison stuff, let's talk about community. They're looking at you like, 'What? What *community*?'"

COMMUNITY OF CAPITAL

People in capitalist society, by and large, are divided against one another. What ties people together is not, in most cases, stable affective ties of love, care, or solidarity, but the impersonal domination of prices and exchanges. Some Marxists refer to this alienation, this erosion of community, as "separation." The dominant community in which we live is a community of capital. Capitalism constitutes an interdependent web of social relations characterized by market dependency, by the necessity of selling to survive. Most people sell their labor power or whatever is available to them, as more informal workers; capitalists sell products and services. We are all enmeshed in markets.

The structure of universal market dependency is mediated by direct personal relationships. Those who can't find a job can partner and depend on someone else who has one. This usually takes the form of the nuclear family or other forms of private households. Dependency on the private household to survive leaves people vulnerable to interpersonal partner violence, abusive relationships, terrible childhoods, and other issues of concern to those pursuing accountability and transformative justice. Of course, market dependency creates this same vulnerability to abuse within the workplace as well.

Community can rarely be adequate to our hopes under capitalism; it is simply not congruent with the actually existing web of human interdependency. This web, constituted by the domination of impersonal market forces, or instantiated directly within the dictatorship of the workplace, can never offer a community. This is not just because it is too cruel or too oppressive, it is also because it is always mystified, opaque, and alienated.

All other collectivities, insofar as they do not overlap with actually existing practices of material survival, are readily torn apart as each participant must seek a means of self-reproduction. Because a core activity of collective human life is so absorbed into market relations, non-market relations become hollow, shallow, and fragile. You may love your friends, but you still have to pay rent. Your community may provide housing for some months or years—through a rental party, friends offering you their couch, an independent autonomous squat, a generous roommate—but in a capitalist society, eventually you will do what it takes to go out and find a job or attach yourself in an isolating couple form to someone with housing to offer. Because property relations form the basis of stable communities, those who do not own property face the constant risk of losing a community adequate to meeting shared emotional needs.

FANTASY OF COMMUNITY

If our experience of community is overwhelmingly disappointing, fragile, or fleeting, why, then, do we talk about it so much?

Miranda Joseph, in *Against the Romance of Community*, uses Jacques Derrida and Marx to question the ideological project of nonprofits—also termed non-governmental organizations, community-based organizations, and the voluntary sector. Much like accountability, nonprofits derive their legitimacy from reference to community. She writes,

> Insofar as the "good" provided by nonprofits is "community," nonprofits do not merely complement the market and the state but rather mark the absent center of capitalism. . . . The common name, the fear-inspired name, for this absence of desire for, of consent to, the "free and fair" process by which capitalism distributes power and wealth to some while diminishing the power and wealth of others, an absence of subjects properly constituted as voluntary participants in capitalism is, of course, Communism. Nonprofits make this absence present, but they give it another name, the name Community.[1]

At its worst, community serves as an obscuring fantasy, a fiction we use to psychologically protect ourselves from the horror and despair of life under capitalism. We seize upon a given group of friends, a snapshot of a momentarily vibrant social world, and hope it can last. As it erodes, we set out to find another, or to patch it up where we can. Community serves as an ideological fiction, covering over the relentless harm of capitalist social relations and cruel state policies. It is the fantasy space for a collectivity forged through deliberate willed voluntarism, whether in the form of organizing a late-night dance party, a socialist party, or a block party. Each may form a community temporarily, but claiming it as such keeps at bay the fear it will soon be torn apart. When deployed by liberals or elite-class forces, the language of community can be a cruel deception that ultimately promotes the very forces which systematically render it impossible.

ABOLITION

Accountability, transformative justice, and restorative justice are often rooted in a politics of abolition, specifically the abolition of prisons and police. Recognizing the court system, the prison-industrial complex, and police as sources of violent harm, these frameworks seek out new ways of addressing conflict. As the underlying political commitment of much accountability work, police and prison abolition are invaluable.

Yet under the banner of prison and police abolition, we identify a few interconnected but distinct projects, all closely related to the meanings of accountability.

First, dominant in prison abolitionism is a commitment to *decarceration*. Mass incarceration has been a devastating horror for working-class Black and brown people, destroying the lives of millions. Much of Critical Resistance's organizing has focused on halting new jail and prison construction, opposing prison reforms that provide political cover to expand incarceration, and pushing for policy reforms to reduce prison populations. Admirably, abolitionist organizing for decarceration has often engaged the leadership of formerly and currently incarcerated people. It has also fostered crucial analysis on the causes and dynamics of mass incarceration and associated industries, as exemplified in Ruth Wilson Gilmore's book *Golden Gulag*, referenced in our introduction. Mass incarceration is a relatively recent phenomena—on the rise since the 1970s, concurrent with neoliberalism—and prison abolition is the main political articulation of a commitment to bringing this era of mass incarceration to an end.

Second, prison and police abolitionism often refer to an ethical stance in the present, a practice in relating to other people. This often includes an orientation toward transformative justice and a challenge to relating to others in a punitive way, opposed to labeling people as toxic or altogether bad. As part of not incarcerating *anyone*, this ethical stance often includes voicing public opposition to incarcerating high-profile perpetrators of violence, including those who are widely and justly hated. Abolitionism as an ethical stance is a rejection of the "cop in our heads and hearts"—a movement slogan echoed by our interviewees, which is also a call for personal transformation to become more principled, loving, and effective revolutionaries.

Third, prison and police abolition are a *revolutionary horizon*. Prison abolitionists periodically recognize that eliminating prisons altogether would require a wholesale transformation in our economy, including meeting people's basic needs. It is through abolition that activists today most often talk of revolution and what may come after. Prison and police abolition offer the most widely shared revolutionary horizon in current mass struggles. Drawing on the rich legacy of anti-prison activists, it was then taken up in the waves of popular and insurrectionary movements through Black Lives Matter and the George Floyd uprising. It also offers one of the most substantial original contributions made by the current era of struggle to revolutionary theory. In the political conceptions of many advocates, police and prison abolition would be the fulfillment of the long history of Black freedom struggle and is inseparable with trans and queer liberation.

Yet much remains undertheorized in understanding prison or police abolition as a revolutionary horizon. Though mass incarceration and modern policing are relatively recent phenomena, they are the latest iterations of other forms of institutionalized class violence. Throughout the entire long history of private property and class society, there have been (in Lenin's paraphrasing of Engels) "special bodies of armed men." Police and prison expansion have been enabled in part by popular anxieties about violence and harm, leading activists to correctly point out that neither police nor prisons actually contribute to our safety. But police and prisons do not primarily exist to address conflicts of interpersonal harm. They exist as the latest iteration of a millenia-old commitment to the use of violence to defend class rule. Under capitalism, the armed defense of private property (and hence, class domination) has primarily taken the form of the modern state, with its accompanying institutions of modern policing.

The history of state socialism in the twentieth century makes it clear that not all self-identified communists recognize the need to destroy the modern state as the substantiation of the rule of capital, suggesting the historic need to develop an abolitionist critique over recent decades. However, we are unable to imagine prison abolition without the concurrent overcoming of the property form. The connection between prison abolition and communism remains grossly undertheorized and underspecified. Some abolitionists, like Gilmore or Angela Davis, are thoroughly rooted in Marxism, and no doubt understand prison abolition as a means to overcoming private property and the state. For others, however, this is far less clear.

Strangely, we find that the crucial point—that prison abolition would require overcoming class society—is almost never directly stated. This has let abolition sometimes take the place of a substantive anti-capitalist critique. We have seen, at times, people discussing police and prison abolition as if there could be a set policy reform implemented under the existing capitalist state. This is clearly mistaken. Even with much-needed victories in defunding the police or dismantling mass incarceration, the capitalist class will make sure armed men continue to exist to defend their property. Only a revolution, with the defeat of the capitalist state and collective seizure of the means of production, could provide the basis for eliminating police altogether.

For all the major theoretical advances they offer to all revolutionaries today, prison and police abolition have largely developed after the collapse of other vibrant theoretical and political revolutionary frameworks and movements. Many anarchists, communists, and Black revolutionary nationalists turned to prison abolitionist organizing precisely because it was a way they could continue to talk about revolution in the long reactionary period that has coincided with the expansion of mass incarceration—a period when discussing revolutionary politics became especially difficult. Incarcerated people and their families faced the most brutal brunt of this reactionary era, characterized by the expansion of mass incarceration. Political prisoners, persistent in their organizing and militant resistance, acted as a politicized core to many anti-prison movements, often linking to earlier eras of insurgency. It was through a focus on prisons that something of a revolutionary horizon could survive.

Prison and police abolition (as the dispensing with the existence of "special bodies of armed men") and communism (as the overcoming of class society) depend on each other. That they have developed as theoretic frameworks in a strange separation—despite many important theorists and activists clearly being committed to both—is an important historical puzzle and a major obstacle to the advance of our movements. To understand police and prison abolition as constituting a dimension of communist revolution is to explore their connection to a whole set of questions that have concerned theories of revolution: debates over the roles of diverse phenomena, including disciplined parties, mass democratic organizations, the contexts of war and severe economic crisis, transitional institutions, and violence in the revolutionary process. We understand prison abolition as a crucial contribution to a broader effort to conceive of, theorize, and fight for a free society, alongside and inseparable from a thoroughgoing critique of private property, class society, and capitalism.

ASPIRATIONS OF COMMUNITY

Often when we speak of community, we are also speaking of our own hopes for what the world can be. Though we may be mistaken about the resiliency or depth of our current social relationships, we are speaking a fantasy that expresses our political desire. Community, at its best, is our aspiration for genuine interdependence, mutual effective care, and a shared collectivity of human flourishing. We speak of community as if it has already arrived, as if it is at hand.

This community we imagine is one adequate to our aspirations: We imagine it capable of holding each other accountable, mediating our conflicts, helping us to become better people. We yearn for community as a moral force balancing and reconciling individual freedom and collective well-being. We imagine what Martin Luther King Jr. called "the beloved community"—the one generations of activists have tried to build and maintain in radical social movements.

As we've argued here, this aspiration for community has proved disappointing. What is often missing from this aspiration is the recognition that such a community would necessitate control over the means of production. Under capitalism, every individual has to balance their aspired accountability to the community and their actually existing and necessary accountability to their employer and to broader market demands. Only when the means of material reproduction and survival are either freely and universally available or under collective control of a community can community serve the functions we ask of it. It is easy to think of many fascist, feudal, and authoritarian collectivist regimes that integrate material survival into community in horrific ways, often under the guise of moral tutelage. But a true community, a community that meets the aspirations placed on the phrase "beloved community," could exist only under communism. This community of communism depends on both the universal and unconditional availability of the means of sustaining life, and the democratic and collective management of the means of production. The realization of our hopes for community only can be communism.

The career of accountability shows there is an urgently felt need for an alternative way to live with others. The project of abolition builds upon these efforts to implement processes of redress and repair structurally and without state systems and carceral punishments. These practices demonstrate that abolition is a constructive process. On another level, the concept of accountability also provides a haven to protect the necessary belief in the possibility of radical transformation. Historically, this belief has suffered many blows. There is, as some of the interviewees describe, a naive belief in transformation as an instance of abused logic: "This time, things will be different." But this is not a counsel of inaction or despair. In fact, it is only through recognizing the fundamental limits to action that a critical strategy of transformation can finally succeed.

1

Miranda Joseph, *Against the Romance of Community*
(Minneapolis: University of Minnesota Press, 2002), 73.

Black, Stephanie, dir., *Life and Debt*, 2001.

Boggs, Grace Lee. "Organization Means Commitment (Commitment Is the Key)." 1972.

Creative Interventions. *Creative Interventions Toolkit: A Practical Guide to Stop Interpersonal Violence*. n.p., 2012.

Critical Resistance. *Resources for Addressing Harm, Accountability, and Healing*. Accessed April 2, 2023, https://criticalresistance.org/addressing-harm-accountability-andhealing/.

Davis, Mike. "Hell Factories in the Fields." *Nation*, February 20, 1995.

Gilmore, Ruth Wilson. *Golden Gulag: Prisons, Surplus, Crisis, and Opposition in Globalizing California*. Berkeley: University of California Press, 2007.

Freedom Road Socialist Organization, "On the Crisis of Socialism." May 1991, https://www.marxists.org/history/erol/ncm-7/fr-crisis.pdf/.

In the Belly: An Abolitionist Journal 1 (May 2020).

Joseph, Miranda. *Against the Romance of Community*. Minneapolis: University of Minnesota Press, 2002.

Kaba, Mariame, and Shira Hassan. *Fumbling Towards Repair: A Workbook for Community Accountability Facilitators*. Chicago: Project NIA, Just Practice, 2019.

Liberation Road. "Points of Unity on Gender Liberation." Accessed April 2, 2023, https://roadtoliberation.org/points-ofunity-on-gender-liberation/.

Morris, Mark, ed. *Instead of Prisons: A Handbook for Abolitionists*. Syracuse, NY: Prison Research Education Action Project, 1976.

Schulman, Sarah. *Conflict Is Not Abuse: Overstating Harm, Community Responsibility, and the Duty of Repair*. Vancouver: Arsenal Pulp Press, 2016.

Stahl, Aviva. "Trust in Instinct." *New Inquiry*, May 9, 2017, https://thenewinquiry.com/trust-in-instinct/.

Team Colors Collective (Craig Hughes, Stevie Peace, and Kevin Van Meter), eds. *Uses of a Whirlwind: Movement, Movements, and Contemporary Radical Currents in the United States*. Edinburgh: AK Press, 2010.

Abolition and Social Work
Possibilities, Paradoxes, and the Practice of Community Care
Edited by Mimi E. Kim, Cameron Rasmussen, and Durrell M.
Washington, foreword by Mariame Kaba

Abolition Feminisms Vol. 1
Organizing, Survival, and Transformative Practice
Edited by Alisa Bierria, Jakeya Caruthers, and Brooke Lober
Foreword by Dean Spade

All Our Trials
Prisons, Policing, and the Feminist Fight to End Violence
(Revised Edition) Emily L. Thuma, foreword by Sarah Haley

Country Queers: A Love Letter
Rae Garringer

Loving in the War Years: And Other Writings, 1978-1999
Cherríe Moraga

Not Your Rescue Project: Migrant Sex Workers Fighting for Justice
Chanelle Gallant and Elene Lam, afterword by Robyn Maynard,
foreword by Harsha Walia

Saving Our Own Lives: A Liberatory Practice of Harm Reduction
Shira Hassan, foreword by adrienne maree brown, introduction by
Tourmaline

So We Can Know: Writers of Color on Pregnancy, Loss, Abortion, and Birth
Edited by Aracelis Girmay

We Grow the World Together: Parenting Toward Abolition
Edited by Maya Schenwar and Kim Wilson